My Giant Life

My Giant Life

LAWRENCE TAYLOR

with WILLIAM WYATT

Library of Congress Cataloging-in-Publication Data

Names: Taylor, Lawrence, 1959- author.
Title: My Giant life / Lawrence Taylor.
Description: Chicago, Illinois : Triumph Books LLC, [2016]
Identifiers: LCCN 2016020749 | ISBN 9781629372525
Subjects: LCSH: Taylor, Lawrence, 1959- | Football players—United States—
    Biography. | Linebackers (Football)—United States—Biography. | New York
    Giants (Football team)—History.
Classification: LCC GV939.T34 A3 2016 | DDC 796,332092 [B] —dc23 LC
record available at https://lccn.loc.gov/2016020749

This book is available in quantity at special discounts for your group or organization. For further information, contact:

Triumph Books LLC
814 North Franklin Street
Chicago, Illinois 60610
(312) 337-0747
www.triumphbooks.com

Printed in U.S.A.
ISBN: 978-1-62937-252-5
Design by Alex Lubertozzi
Page production by Meghan Grammer
Photos courtesy of AP Images unless otherwise noted

To Giants fans

Praise for Lawrence Taylor

"You saw hunger [in Taylor's eyes]. Some guys were great at playing their position but didn't have that feeling inside, and that was something that L.T. had with him every down of every game and he never lost it." —*Hall of Fame NFL quarterback Joe Montana*

"I don't expect to see another player as great as Lawrence Taylor. Forget all that talk about impact players...this guy personally won games for the New York Giants. If you're looking for the best way to describe him, try this: he did it every play, every game." —*Former Giants coach Ray Perkins*

"L.T. set the standard with his speed, his strength, his all-out play. A lot of players have tried to copy his style, but there will never be another L.T." —*Hall of Fame NFL safety Larry Wilson*

"He was the No. 2 pick and could have come in with a big-headed attitude. But he came in eager to learn. By the way, anybody that big shouldn't be that fast." —*Former Giants linebacker Brian Kelley*

"In 30 or 40 years, I'm going to take out the tapes and show them to my grandkids. To show them I really played against Lawrence Taylor. The greatest. That he was everything they said he was." —*Former NFL running back Keith Byars*

"We put three guys on him. It didn't seem to matter. He always made an impact." —*Former NFL quarterback Neil Lomax*

"We had to try in some way to have a special game plan just for Lawrence Taylor. Now, you didn't do that very often in this league, but I think he's one person that we learned the lesson the hard way. We lost ball games." —*Former NFL coach Joe Gibbs*

"I mean everything you did [on offense] was predicated to where he was and what he was doing." —*Hall of Fame quarterback John Elway*

"Lawrence Taylor, defensively, has had as big an impact as any player I've ever seen. He changed the way defense is played, the way pass-rushing is played, the way linebackers play and the way offenses block linebackers." —*Hall of Fame NFL coach and TV analyst John Madden*

"All I can say about Lawrence Taylor is that he's the best defensive football player I've seen. I've said many times he's the best player I've seen in my era defensively. Everyone else is a pretender." —*Hall of Fame NFL defensive end Howie Long*

"I think that he was the greatest football player that I ever stepped on the field against. Nobody dictated what you could do offensively like L.T." —*Former NFL quarterback Steve Bartkowski*

"He is the Michael Jordan of football." —*Former Giants defensive lineman George Martin*

"There are priority positions in this game, quarterback is one of those, so I consider that. But if you're pinning me down—I'm a little preju-diced—I think I'd take Lawrence Taylor.... Because I know he's going to be there every Sunday and try his best to win, for sure." —*Former NFL coach Bill Parcells, when asked by Fox Sports who would be the one player he'd pick if he were starting a football team*

"There's no other linebacker who had that air about him. When you think of linebackers, you think of L.T. You can think of [Dick] Butkus, you can think of everybody, but when you say 'L.T.,' it makes every-body raise their heads." —*Former Giants linebacker Jessie Armstead*

"Everybody uses L.T. as the measuring stick. I hear comments all the time, 'This guy is going to be the next L.T.' Those guys never seem to measure up.... Not everybody can be L.T., with the size and speed and quickness. But you can use that to show, 'This is what it's supposed to look like.'" —*Former Giants linebackers coach Mike Haluchak*

"If there ever was a Superman in the NFL, I think he wore No. 56 for the Giants." —*Former NFL quarterback Joe Theismann*

"L.T. is that person who wants to be portrayed living on the edge. Lawrence is the guy who came in from Williamsburg [Virginia], very humble, very caring. L.T. is a star. L.T. is what probably has gotten Lawrence in all of the stuff because Lawrence is a sweetheart. I don't really deal with L.T. I deal with Lawrence." —*Former Giants linebacker Harry Carson*

"I had to cut L.T. on one play, and I cut him flat. He got up and came at me. 'Don't you ever cut me again,' L.T. said. I said, 'Okay.' When I went back to the bench, they said they wanted me to cut Taylor again. I said, 'No, you'll have to get somebody else. I promised.'" —*Hall of Fame running back Eric Dickerson, on his rookie-season experience with Lawrence Taylor*

"If there's pressure on the defense anywhere, it's opposite Lawrence because most offenses are geared to go away from him. So if you're not ready, they're going to have a field day on your side." —*Former Giants linebacker Carl Banks*

CONTENTS

INTRODUCTION

B ecause I was an athlete, I could have played a lot of different sports. Athletes can do that sort of thing because sports come easy to them. I could have played baseball; I just wasn't crazy about the game. There's too much standing around in baseball, not enough action. On the other hand, football brought plenty of action—and it also brought the hitting.

I started playing football when I was a junior in high school and I just got better and better every year. Football has a physical component that I just loved. I don't know about a lot of things in life. But I know football.

When I was drafted in the NFL in 1981, I stepped straight from the University of North Carolina into the action. I wanted contact every day. I just wanted to hit, hit, hit. And on Sundays, I dominated from the beginning, playing the position of linebacker like nobody had ever played it before. I did things in the game that nobody had ever seen. A lot of people said I redefined the position during my years with the New York Giants.

Giants general manager George Young said this about me: "He had an immediate impact. He made the weakside linebacker position the designated pass rusher position. Before L.T., the glamour guys were the inside guys. You could name a lot of middle line-backers: [Dick] Butkus, Mike Curtis, Ray Nitschke. But how many

XVI | My Giant Life

outside linebackers could you name?

"The first thing quarterbacks would do after they broke the huddle is say, 'Where is this guy?' Lawrence is a guy who's had many pretenders. Every time a new guy comes out, his agent says, 'This is the next L.T.' I say, 'There is only one No. 56.'"

"Redefining the position" wasn't high on my list of priorities. I wanted to play the game. I wanted to dominate. I wanted to win. The things I could do, those were talents given to me from the man upstairs. For example, while running backs and tight ends weren't strong enough to take me on, tackles weren't quick enough for me. Even when the offense went to different combinations of blockers, they still couldn't stop me from getting busy in their backfield. I guess I was a freak.

Bill Parcells' understanding combined with my talent allowed me to do some things that weren't scripted. That led to a lot of good Sunday afternoons for the New York Giants. Am I the best defensive player ever? I know I'm up there, but that's tough for me to say. I played in a different era and a different time. Some things I could do, other players couldn't, and there certainly were players who could do things I couldn't.

I'm not really sure I know how to explain my career. I felt like a man playing with boys, and the things I could do, naturally, people were in awe of. I just know I always wanted to be the best at what I was doing. Parcells was our defensive coordinator my rookie season. He could see that I had the talent to do anything I wanted. As a coach, the most important thing he had to do with regard to me was to try to channel those instincts in the right direction. A lot of that came down to things like making sure that I understood when I could gamble and when I couldn't. Or making sure I knew how to play the draw when the other team tried to counter my aggressiveness. Stuff like that.

The New Orleans Saints had the first pick of the NFL draft the year I came out of college. Their coach, Bum Phillips, had Earl Campbell when he coached the Oilers. Campbell had been a bruising running back and carried the Oilers' offense. Phillips was hoping to catch lightning in a bottle for a second time when he drafted George Rogers, who had won the Heisman Trophy at South Carolina.

I really don't know what might have happened in my career if the Saints had taken me instead of Rogers. Going to the Giants probably turned out to be one of the luckiest breaks of my life, because they were rebuilding. Part of that rebuilding effort dealt with going to another defensive scheme. Fortunately, Parcells became the guy designated to come up with and implement that scheme.

People weren't used to the kind of football I brought to the league. Linebackers were simply linebackers until I came along. Typical linebackers stopped the run and defended the pass. Once Parcells evaluated me, he began to let me do different things. I could rush the quarterback. At times I didn't even know what defense we were in or what the offense was doing, but I always told the coaches, "When I make mistakes, good things come of it."

All the while, I kept playing a physical game. I grasped the fact early that the nastiest, meanest players were the ones who got the furthest in the league. So I never had time to offer condolences when I put a lick on someone. I didn't play dirty, but I needed that to keep the edge.

We had a good group of linebackers when I got to the Giants and some other quality players as well. I think my arrival helped rejuvenate that group's desire to win. Guys such as Brad Van Pelt and Harry Carson were talented players who had played for losing teams for so long they almost accepted defeat. I mean, the Giants had gone through eight straight losing seasons to that point and had not made the playoffs in 18 seasons. So I think they were able to rediscover what it was like to be a player who refused to take losing lightly. And we began to win—a lot.

Because of the things I could do and the way I played, I earned a lot of honors along the way, such as the league's MVP award in

1986. I was a three-time Defensive Player of the Year, earned 10 Pro Bowl berths, was named a member of the league's 75th-anniversary team selected in 1994, and earned a spot in the Hall of Fame in Canton. Most importantly, I played for two Super Bowl–winning teams. None of those accomplishments could have been attained without having a bunch of teammates who could play, too.

I played within the rules for the sake of the game. But that didn't mean I couldn't ramp up the intensity a little bit. Whenever I threw up before a game, I felt like I would have a big day. If your eyes got red and you got that sick stomach, you knew you were ready. I experienced a handful of games during my career where I felt like all of the action shifted to slow motion. On those days I felt like I could be out there all day, totally in the zone, where I didn't even know where I was on the field. Everything was just totally blocked out. And I could do no wrong.

As a player, you understood there were situations that affected the momentum of the game. I felt as though you had to be able to recognize those situations and make plays.

During my rookie year, we went to St. Louis to play the Cardinals with two games left in the season. We could smell the playoffs, but we needed to finish strong. I remember blitzing their quarterback, Neil Lomax, from his blind side. After I leaped over a blocker I slammed right into Lomax, which caused him to fumble the ball. George Martin scooped up the ball and ran it back for a touchdown. I knew Lomax couldn't see me when I went inside instead of outside, which I usually did. I'll always remember that as one of my best hits. I couldn't believe it when Lomax got up from that one.

Probably the game I'm most proud of was the one we played against the Saints in New Orleans in 1988. I suited up even though I had a torn muscle in my chest. I had to wear a shoulder harness, but I still played and actually came away with three sacks and two forced fumbles. We won on a last-minute 35-yard field goal by Paul McFadden. Afterward, Parcells gave me a hug and told me, "You were great tonight. I don't know how you got through that." I told him, "Me neither."

I would love to have a do-over for the '87 team after we won our first Super Bowl. I'm sure a lot of my teammates probably feel that way, too, because success went to our heads. After we won the thing, everybody wanted to write a book and nobody wanted to work anymore. Seemed like everybody wanted to redo their contract, too. We screwed that up. There was no way that team shouldn't have come back and won more Super Bowls. Success is intoxicating, though. And that's what makes consistency in any sport so hard.

I admire teams that can find a way to do it every year. Take the New England Patriots; they find a way to do it every year. Back in the day you had to admire the Denver Broncos and the Buffalo Bills, teams that found a way to get back to the show each season. And they did it every year when the pressure was on. That's tough to do.

Do I miss football? I do not.

People always told me I'd get the feeling that I wanted to play again, but I never have. I just moved on to other things. I did enjoy the game while I played it, though. I loved the game. I loved the contact. I still do love the game of football and what the game has done for me. As I get older, I really don't have any regrets. I'm not the kind of guy who looks back and says, "I wish I would have done things this way or that way." Or, "I wish I hadn't gotten into trouble." All of that's part of the growing process. What I went through made me stronger.

I mean, it wasn't an easy road. Actually, I traveled a pretty rocky road. I can say this: the things that I've done weren't to hurt anybody. Those things hurt me. I've never tried to sugarcoat any of the stuff I did, or hide anything when I told my kids about the stuff I'd done. You hope as a parent that if you tell them the truth, you might spare them some of the embarrassment and pain that you went through. Having taken that road I'm equipped to handle the tough stuff that comes up every day. Bad things are going to happen. But xx | My Giant Life

I feel lucky to have played when I did and lucky to be around the people who helped shape who I was—guys such as Parcells and Bill Belichick. Wellington Mara always looked out for me. I made so many friends while I was on the Giants, particularly with all the guys who played alongside me at linebacker. That crew I played with—I'll tell you what, most every linebacker I ever played with was a class person. We still hang together. We still talk to one another. Carl Banks, Harry Carson, Brian Kelley, Pepper Johnson, Gary Reasons. We all still talk and still love each other and reminisce about the good old days. Some I remember, but I don't remember what year I played with them, still I really enjoyed being around those guys. But the core guys, the guys you could count on every Sunday, the guys that were the backbone of your team, everybody has them, we're still together. We're a close-knit group. What we did to get to the championship helped build those bonds.

The fans treated me well and I love how they still treat me. I'm more appreciative of the fans from where I sit now than I once had been. Giants fans were always the best fans in the league, too. They supported me always. I can't thank them enough for all the support they gave me or express how pumped up I used to get when they'd be chanting "L-T! L-T!" Seeing so many of them wearing No. 56 jerseys, and the banners they made, all of that was good stuff. Our fans were a big part of our success. You can ask anybody I played with about that.

How am I remembered? People remember me the way they want to. That was never for me to decide. I do know what I accomplished. I went to Super Bowls and the playoffs. I earned the respect of players in the league and people around the country. People who study the game, the players I played against—and some of the players since—know what I did. You know as a player it's all going to be over at some point in time. So it's all about what type of impact you had on the game. To me, that was the most important thing, knowing that I made a difference in the game. And I'm happy I did.

My Giant Life

CHAPTER 1

THE BEGINNING

DRAFTED SECOND
BY THE GIANTS

George Young wanted to select me with the second pick of the 1981 NFL Draft.

Young worked as the Giants' general manager at the time, and the team wasn't any good. I later learned that the days leading up to that draft were some of Young's most stressful.

Word was he'd grown enamored with me after watching me play against Clemson my senior year at North Carolina. A big part of that had to do with the time I spent in the other team's backfield. I saw a statistic from my senior season that 38 of my 69 tackles happened in the other team's backfield, including 16 sacks. That helped us go 11–1 that season while earning me Atlantic Coast Conference Player of the Year honors—along with Young's favor. Problem was, the Saints had the top pick.

Everybody knew that the Saints liked South Carolina running back George Rogers. He'd won the Heisman Trophy that year, and Saints coach Bum Phillips thought he could be another Earl Campbell, who had been Phillips' horse when he coached the Houston Oilers from 1975 through 1980. He wanted to make a splash in his first season with the Saints and he saw Rogers as the guy to help take him in that direction.

Rogers stood 6'2", 220 pounds, and averaged six yards a carry for the Gamecocks while leading the nation in rushing.

Phillips believed in a strong running game being able to help an ailing defense. As he told *The Sporting News* prior to the draft, "The best way to help your defense is to keep it off the field. If you've got a good running game, you use about three times the amount of time as you do passing the ball, because every time you miss a pass, you stop the clock. With a good running game, a 40-or 50-yard drive from your own 20 will eat up five, six, maybe seven minutes and put you in a position to punt them into a hole."

Of course, every plan has a fallback in the NFL, so the Giants had to prepare themselves for the possibility that the Saints might reverse fields and decide to draft me.

Leading up to the draft, the Saints had me come to New Orleans, and I must have made an impression during the visit because I heard their defensive coaches tried to convince Phillips that he needed to draft me with the first pick.

Back in New York, some of the Giants' defensive players were not particularly enamored with the idea that the team would select another linebacker. Looking back, I can't really blame them. They already had a pretty nice group of linebackers with Harry Carson, Brad Van Pelt, and Brian Kelley. The team had gone 4–12 and really needed a running back to help keep some of the heat off quarterback Phil Simms. In addition, those guys knew I'd be getting a big contract. They weren't happy, so they threatened to walk out.

Upon learning about the problems I might be facing with my future Giants teammates, my agent, Mike Trope, and I sent telegrams to the Giants. Mine went to head coach Ray Perkins and Mike's went to Young. We told them if I got picked by the Giants, I wouldn't play for them.

I heard they threw those telegrams in the trash.

Perkins visited me in Chapel Hill before the draft. We watched film together and at some point during that film session he decided he was good with me. I was wearing shorts and a T-shirt so I could work out for them. But Perkins said he didn't need me to do that. We went to dinner later, and that's when he told me I would become a New York Giant.

Later we threatened that I'd play in the Canadian Football League. In addition, the possibility that the Saints might trade their pick continued to exist right up until the draft.

The Dallas Cowboys wanted me, but they knew that the only way they could get me would be to draft in front of the Giants. According to reports, they offered the Saints defensive end Larry Bethea, running back Ron Springs, linebacker Guy Brown, and their No. 1 pick (26th overall) for their No. 1 draft pick. Phillips wouldn't go for it.

On Tuesday, April 28, 1981, the Saints picked George Rogers with the first pick. The Giants were next and my name was called out as their selection at No. 2.

I think the Saints finally decided the morning of the draft that they wanted Rogers, which ended up being a good decision for me because I had my career in New York. I never looked back after that.

Once the Giants selected me, I made the following statement about becoming the team's first-round pick:

"I'm happy to be going to New York, because it's one of the greatest cities in the world. There's so many people who can see you and appreciate you. That's one of the greatest things that can happen to me. I hope to bring the New York people a winner, because that's something they deserve."

I apologized to the Giants for the telegraph I'd sent them. When I spoke to Perkins, I told him I used poor judgment in sending the thing. And some of the players called me and we got straight. Some of what I thought was going on wasn't.

Rogers ended up leading the league in rushing with 1,674 yards in his first season. At the time, that stood as a rookie record. He also was selected as the NFL Rookie of the Year.

Things turned out well for me, too.

When I got there, I was thinking, *if y'all don't want me, just trade me somewhere else.* But after watching me practice for about 10 minutes everybody thought that drafting me was the right move to make.

I was very fortunate to be drafted by the Giants. I see guys who played in the league a long time. They walk around their town and nobody knows them. People know me in New York. I enjoy the area. I'm treated very well. It's just like the TV show *Cheers.* You want to go someplace where everybody knows your name.

New York is that for me.

ROOKIE SEASON

Heading into my rookie season in the NFL, there seemed to be a lot of rules specifying what I could and couldn't do. In college I pretty much had the freedom to do what I wanted and I didn't have to be in a specific area on every play.

During the exhibition season, I managed to lead the team in sacks, with four, but I was limited to certain situations when I was allowed to rush the passer. I wanted to rush the passer more. I also remember wanting to fit in with the established group of linebackers on that team. So I resigned myself to the fact that if they wanted me to play the pass, I would play the pass.

I wanted to be in great shape my first season so I could play to the best of my ability to help the team win. I was driven to be the best. I wanted to be everything I could possibly be and even make All-Pro.

Ray Perkins was our coach in 1981. He told me I got too aggressive at times and that I needed to get the big picture before I committed myself one way or the other. During the exhibition season, I made mistakes I knew I shouldn't have made—such as my pass drops.

Dropping back into the areas I needed to get to for pass coverage wasn't the problem. Reading the keys took some time getting used to, though, like when the Steelers got the best of me on a flea flicker in our final preseason game. Still, I felt pretty good about my progress by the time the regular season started. I felt like I was getting better in each game.

The mental approach to the NFL brought another adjustment for me. We'd had a fairly simple defense at North Carolina compared with what we were doing with the Giants. A lot of times those blackboard diagrams and rolling zones were dizzying. I'd take home film and learn as much as I could because I felt like the more I knew, the better I'd play. Physically, I couldn't have been much better at the time. I stood 6'4", 240 pounds and ran a 4.6 in the 40. Players of my size simply weren't supposed to run that damn fast.

As far as the team I'd joined, the Giants had plenty of talent—particularly on defense and the linebackers in our 3–4 defense: Harry Carson, Brian Kelley, Brad Van Pelt, and me. That's a hell of a group to begin my career with.

Unfortunately, the team had not had a winning season since 1972 and they'd only gone 8–6 that season. That reality left Giants fans starving for a winner. As for the players, I saw plenty of talent on our team, but it didn't seem like anybody really knew how to win yet. They'd gone 4–12 in 1980 and were outscored 425–249.

Entering the 1981 season, the Giants' record against the Eagles personified the frustration. Our NFC East rival had defeated us in 11 straight games. So when we opened with the Eagles at the Meadowlands, everybody in our locker room wanted to beat their ass.

But the opener turned out to be more of the same.

Billy Taylor fumbled right before halftime, setting up an Eagles field goal that gave them a 10–3 lead. Ron Jaworski put the dagger into us in the third quarter when he connected on a 55-yard touchdown pass to Rodney Parker. Up until then, no Eagles wide receivers had caught a pass all day. That one put us down 17–3. Combined with a weak ground game that saw us gain only 55 yards in 23 carries, what took place added up to a 24–10 loss, giving the Eagles their 12th consecutive win against us.

Even with the offense misfiring, we had some chances to get back in that game. For example, in the second quarter when Jaworski threw behind his receiver at the Eagles' 23 and Van Pelt was right there. But he couldn't hang on to the ball, turning what could have been a pick six into nothing. I remember Jaworski kept arguing with the refs. One time he asked them, "Where's the flag?" That's when I pointed up and said, "The flag's in the stands."

We went on the road to play the Redskins the following week and came away 17–7 winners before returning home to play the Saints. That one probably got a little more hyped up than it should have been because the Saints had George Rogers, the No. 1 pick in the NFL Draft that year, and I was No. 2, so the media made it out to be almost like a heavyweight fight: Rogers vs. Taylor. Alas, the game turned out to be more about Phil Simms. He completed 28-of-41 passes for 324 yards and a touchdown, and we beat the Saints 20–7.

Most thought Rogers and I both played well. He ran the ball 20 times for 75 yards and I had three tackles. One of those tackles came on a fourth down in the third quarter when I stopped Rogers.

We seemed to keep gaining confidence throughout the season before finding ourselves at 5–6 when we headed to Philadelphia to play our longtime nemesis. The Eagles stood at 9–2 and were looking strong, so we knew Veterans Stadium would be rocking.

Kelly, Van Pelt and Carson were the only guys on the team who had suffered through all of the 12 consecutive losses to the Eagles, but we still needed to break through that invisible barrier of not being able to beat them.

We were 9 ½-point underdogs going into that game. Simms couldn't play since he'd separated his shoulder and was out for the season, so Scott Brunner started for us. Our running game helped compensate for the loss of Simms. We had improved a lot after acquiring fullback Rob Carpenter from the Houston Oilers.

Heading into that game, Brunner had looked pretty good. Then again, he'd be facing an Eagles front all day that consisted of Claude Humphrey, Dennis Harrison, Kenny Clarke, and Carl Hairston—a tall order for any quarterback, but even more so for one without a lot of experience.

Nevertheless, we came away with a 20–10 win to move to 6–6 on the season and keep our playoff hopes alive.

The big play of the game came in the fourth quarter when Terry Jackson intercepted one of Jaworski's passes and our speedy cornerback returned it 32 yards for a touchdown and a 10-point lead.

We got a little offense that day, too, running a double tight end formation for much of the game. Carpenter ran for 111 yards and Brunner threw for 181 while completing 10 of the 27 passes he threw. That win did a lot for us and got the monkey—uh, Eagle—off our backs.

After beating Philly, we lost to San Francisco before taking a 10–7 win over the Los Angeles Rams. I received probably the highest praise I'd gotten from Perkins after I made a couple of timely plays in that game. I sacked Pat Haden for loss that pushed back Frank Corral's game-tying field-goal attempt to 49 yards, and he missed. Then I intercepted Haden on the Rams' first play of their next possession. Perkins complimented me after that game by saying, "I've never seen any rookie linebacker have a game like that."

A 20–10 win over the St. Louis Cardinals followed by a 13–10 overtime win over the Cowboys gave us a 9–7 record. But we needed a little help if we were going to make the playoffs and that help came from a local source: the Jets.

New York was playing the Packers on the final day of the season, and it worked out such that we needed the Jets to win in order for us to make the playoffs.

Since we'd played the Cowboys on Saturday, everybody watched the Jets–Packers game together the next day at the press lounge inside Giants Stadium. The Jets came through with a 28–3 win to put us into the playoffs. No Giants team had been to the playoffs since 1963, so we were pretty happy.

And who did we see in the playoffs? Of course it would be the guys in green. The way our season had gone, playing the Eagles first seemed like a natural next step.

Fortunately, our bad karma had been repaired by that point.

Philadelphia had two tight ends blocking me that day. That didn't help them much, though; we beat them 27–21 to move us into the division championship against the 49ers. Later I heard that Jaworski said he fumbled at one point in the game, because he'd looked across the line and saw me grinning at him.

Our magical season finally came to an end in San Francisco when the 49ers beat us 38–24.

We had a great run in 1981. That season helped put the foundation in place for future championship teams.

It was a pretty nice rookie season for me, too.

BILL PARCELLS

B ill Parcells is a great coach and one of the best to ever coach any-where. I'm sure he's regarded that way by most.

Bill was the Giants' defensive coordinator my rookie year and he stayed on my ass every play. I couldn't do anything right. I mean, he was tough.

I had a lot of athletic ability. I could do things that nobody else was doing. For example, I might rush the passer and he'd manage to complete a pass to a receiver. Well, then I'd turn around and catch the guy about 20 yards down the field. Or, one minute I'd be rushing and the next minute I'd be intercepting the ball.

But it was always the wrong thing and Bill would say, "You don't do that. You're not supposed to do that." And he just stayed on my ass. After about four or five days of it, I told Bill, "Listen, I don't care if you cut me or if you trade me. I don't care if you put somebody else in here, but you've got to get off my ass because I don't work like that."

Bill told me, "All right, all right, I'll tell you what. I'm going to let you do it your way. But if you screw it up you're going to do it my way." I never had to do it his way.

After that Bill let me do more of my thing and we became the best of friends. Any time I had a problem, I went to him.

Ray Perkins was the head coach of the Giants in 1979 when he offered Bill the position of defensive coordinator, but Bill left before the season started to take another job in Colorado. I think he was just tired of moving around and he didn't want to put his family through a fooball coach's lifestyle any longer.

He called that year away from football "the most miserable year" of his life, and then returned to coaching in 1980 as the New England Patriots' linebackers coach. I mean, what else was he really going to do? Just work at a job punching a clock nine-to-five? Bill was meant to be a coach.

Perkins hired him back on his Giants staff as the defensive coordinator prior to the 1981 season. That worked out well for me, since he changed the defense from a 4–3 to a 3–4 system. The Giants were rebuilding, and I became a big piece of that process.

Parcells knew how to coach a player to learn the system quickly. I followed his lead and good things happened. He could recognize talent, and he'd let that talent flourish. Though he could be a hard-ass, he knew how to have some fun, too. He could give you the needle.

For example, when the Giants selected me with the second pick of the 1981 NFL Draft, the Tampa Bay Buccaneers selected Hugh Green out of Pittsburgh with the seventh pick. Both of us had been down linemen in college.

Based on our skill sets, some thought Green would make a better linebacker than me. The thinking was that he was more refined. One week we were getting ready to play the San Francisco 49ers and we were watching tape of them playing the Bucs, and Parcells asked, "Who's that number 53?" Of course it was Green. And he said, "Man, that guy can play! Wow, he intercepted a pass. We haven't seen that around here." He knew he was getting under my skin.

A week or so later, we were getting ready to play the Los Angeles Rams and were watching film of the Rams against the Bucs. So he started again. "Look at that 53! He's a player! Can you believe what he's doing out there?"

Parcells knew I took the bait, and he still kids me about what happened next. I yelled from the back of the room, "Why didn't you draft that son of a bitch if you liked him that much?"

Everybody laughed.

Perkins left the Giants after the 1982 season to take over as the head coach and athletic director at the University of Alabama. That's when Parcells got the opportunity to become the Giants' head coach, which wasn't exactly easy duty since the team had only one winning season in its previous 10.

We went 3–12–1 in 1983 and a lot of people thought he would get fired.

That turned out to be a really tough year for Bill. Not only did he have to deal with the rumors of getting shown the door, but his parents died the same year.

Fortunately for the Giants, and me, they did not fire Bill. But the organization made changes, and I got a lesson in how teams turn over for talent. The trick all the good coaches know is when to turn over their talent before it's too late. Players get a little wear on the tires, and then it's best to find new ones before the ones you have drag down the team.

After the '83 season, Bill started cleaning house, getting rid of guys that I'd been with since I'd been with the club, such as Brian Kelley and Brad Van Pelt. Those moves really upset me because I was losing friends and, on top of that, I thought those guys were really good players. I was like, "What the hell is going on?"

Bill and I had a talk, and he told me the moves he made were going to make us a better team. I couldn't really see it, given the guys he was bringing in, but his special touch began to show the following season when we went 9–7 and made the playoffs. Then we made the playoffs in 1985 when we went 10–6, giving the organization its first back-to-back playoff appearances since 1961–1963.

In 1986, we went 14–2 during the regular season, and then mowed through the playoffs to the Super Bowl, where we beat the Denver Broncos to become world champions.

Parcells had been right. He had built a hell of a team. And it wasn't until after winning the Super Bowl that we could all look back and recognize that. I don't think we could have gone to our first Super Bowl without a guy like Carl Banks, without a guy like Pepper Johnson. We couldn't have done it. Bill saw that we needed that new talent and he built the team we needed to get there.

I'm forever being asked how good of a coach he was and I'll tell people that he understood football first. And he had a sense for what would work in any given situation. Take that 1986 season; we were playing the Broncos in November at the Meadowlands in a tight game.

Late in that game, we were tied at 16 when Denver defensive end Freddie Gilbert sacked Simms for an 11-yard loss. That left us with a third-and-21 from our own 18. We had the best punter in the league in Sean Landeta, and the wind was at his back. Most coaches would have run the ball up the middle, sent Landeta into the game, punted the thing away, and turned it over to the defense. Not Bill.

Next thing you know, Sims is taking a deep drop. He hung in the pocket until Bobby Johnson got loose in the Broncos secondary and Simms hit him for a 42-yard gain. That play kept the drive that led to Raul Allegre's winning field goal alive.

Bill had balls.

Early in my career, I made a lot of mistakes. When I didn't know what I was doing, my answer to everything was, *If you don't know what you're doing, rush the quarterback.* Bill had enough foresight to let me continue doing what I was doing, though. He could see that even though I was making mistakes, what I did worked.

On top of that, he was a great motivator.

Bill didn't motivate anybody on the team the same way. The way he motivated Simms was different from how he motivated Mark Bavaro. He had about nine different faces he used. That was Bill Parcells' job. He knew what it took to motivate a guy. The stuff he would say to Jumbo Elliott, he wouldn't say to me, because he knew I wouldn't listen to that. Bill knew that everybody didn't respond to the same thing. It was amazing how he could take on 45 different personalities depending on whatever the situation called for.

Simms and Bill used to argue all the time. He knew how Bill operated and perfectly explained some of his genius at working with people in an interview Phil had with Giants.com when he said:

"When I struggled, he'd back off. The better you played, the harder he would be on you. There's a madness to it, because self-satisfaction and all of those things creep into you when you're playing well. In sports the desperate team and desperate player is the guy to look out for. How do you do that to players who are playing well and winning? You have to somehow create a false sense of insecurity or whatever. I guess just keeping them on edge, and that's what he tried to do."

Bill acts like he's dumb, but he's really smart, okay? Seriously, Bill could coach football and he knew people.

Parcells led us to another Super Bowl in 1990. I thought he did a particularly good coaching job that season. We won our first 10 games before finishing 13–3. Along the way, Simms got injured. So Bill had to figure out a way for us to keep it going with our backup quarterback, Jeff Hostetler.

No surprise, we went to more of a ball-control offense and that carried us through the playoffs to the Super Bowl, where we played the high-flying Buffalo Bills. Again, Parcells proved his worth, coming up with a flawless game plan to slow down the Bills. We came away with our second Super Bowl win in as many chances.

Parcells retired after that season, citing health reasons for his decision.

While he was at the helm of the Giants we won three division titles, had just two losing seasons, and went 8–3 in the playoffs.

Nobody ever really thought Bill would give up coaching altogether. And he didn't. He had an offer from the Bucs after the 1991 season. Almost immediately he decided to reject the offer and then he spent his second season with NBC. But after the 1992 season, a year in which the Patriots went 2–14 under Dick MacPherson— a record for which McPherson got fired—the New England Patriots hired Bill.

I laughed when I heard that he'd told the Patriots' owner that he wasn't interested in being competitive. He wanted to bring a championship to New England and if that's what they wanted, he was their guy.

He went 5–11 with the Patriots in 1993 then ran off records of 10–6 and 6–10 before leading them to an 11–5 mark in 1996 en route to the Super Bowl, where they lost to the Packers. That was the year Desmond Howard became the Super Bowl MVP for his 99-yard touchdown return of a kickoff and his 244 all-purpose yards.

Bill left the Patriots for the Jets in 1997 and coached them for three seasons, including a high-water mark of 12–4 in 1998. His final coaching stint came from 2003 through 2006 with the Dallas Cowboys.

Something I always loved about Bill was the fact we pretty much had the same philosophy about football. It's a physical sport, so you have to run the football—especially in Giants country, where it gets cold. And he believed the defense started with the linebackers.

You can't argue with the results he got. He coached the Giants for eight seasons, going 77–49–1, and we had five playoff appearances while he was with us.

In 19 years of coaching, he posted a 172–130–1 mark.

All told, his teams went to three Super Bowls—winning twice— and won three conference championships and five division championships. He finally got his just due when he got enshrined in the Pro Football Hall of Fame in 2013.

That's a pretty strong record for a man who thought about getting out of football, huh? Boy was I fortunate that I started my career with Bill Parcells. For 10 years he was either the defensive coordinator or defensive coach.

People have asked me a lot over the years about my relationship with Bill, and the best way I've answered that question is to say it's like when two people are married for 50 years. You don't have to keep saying, "I love you." It's understood. Whenever anybody brings up Bill Parcells' name to me, it's always going to put a smile on my face. I think the same is true when somebody mentions my name to Bill.

BILL BELICHICK

Bill Belichick is a pain in the ass—a total pain in the ass. No smiling. Driest humor son-of-a-bitch you've ever seen. But that dog knows some football.

The one thing I can say about Belichick is on Sunday afternoon you want to be sitting right beside him. Any other day, you don't want to be near him. But Sunday afternoon, you want to be beside him because he knows what he's doing.

Belichick grew up seemingly destined to become a football coach. I mean, the apple doesn't fall far from the tree.

Bill's father, Steve, was a longtime college football scout and coach. He worked for 34 years at the U.S. Naval Academy. No surprise that Bill would study football with his father, who was not only a father but a coaching mentor. By the time he reached his teenage years, he understood football formations and how to attack defenses better than most coaches.

After graduating from Phillips Academy in Andover, Massachusetts, where he played football and lacrosse, Bill went to Wesleyan University and played football, lacrosse, and squash. Football at Wesleyan isn't going to get you to the next level, but Bill reached the next level when he graduated in 1975. Let's just say he reached the lowest level of the next level. Somehow he landed a job with the Baltimore Colts that paid him $25 a week. Basically, that job required him to do anything head coach Ted Marchibroda wanted.

Subsequently, he worked with the Lions as the special teams coach and by 1978 he was the Broncos' assistant special teams coach and defensive assistant. He joined the Giants in 1979 under Ray Perkins, who was the head coach at the time.

Bill was the assistant special teams coach when I joined the team in 1981. I mean, that's something like a water boy. And he just rose up the next year to special teams coach, and the next year he became the linebackers coach. Then he was defensive coordinator. And when Bill Parcells named him defensive coordinator in 1985, I went into Parcells' office and I asked Bill if he was fucking crazy. Bill explained the situation to me by saying, "Listen, a lot of these defenses we've been running over the years, Bill Belichick designed," and so and so and such and such. And he convinced me eventually that Bill Belichick was the man for the job.

In Belichick's second year as the defensive coordinator in 1986, we had a smothering defense and went on to defeat the Broncos in the Super Bowl.

Bill thrived in the job. He used to tease me about falling asleep in his meetings. My response to that would always be the same: I had to sleep in his meetings because I couldn't sleep in Parcells'.

How good was Bill Belichick? All you have to do is check out the game plan he came up with before we played the Buffalo Bills in Super Bowl XXV.

Jim Kelly led the Bills' offense and they scored points like they were playing a video game. Most of the experts didn't give us a chance to win against them. I couldn't blame them. Hell, they'd scored 95 points in their two playoff games.

You looked at a team like the Buffalo Bills and the one thing that stood out about them was how quickly they would score. It seemed like every three minutes they were scoring a touchdown. We're talking a high-powered offense with four wide receivers, and they operated quickly with no-huddle stuff. None of the teams in the league could handle it.

Belichick came up with a plan where we had two down linemen and the rest were linebackers and defensive backs. We'd been the NFL's best defense against the rush that season. So part of him selling the plan to us was telling us we would win the game if Thurman Thomas gained over 100 yards. Crazy, right? He told us, "Don't worry about Thurman Thomas. You're not going to stop him from getting his yards. Let him get his yards. Fine; let him run. Let him run his ass off all day. We're just going to stop everybody else." And that's what we did.

Kelly was really good, but Belichick didn't think he could read defenses like some of the other top quarterbacks in the league.

That defense Belichick put in shut down everybody else. Now, Thurman Thomas got his yards. He rushed for 100-plus yards. But back in those days, we played great in the red area. We could play the cover two better than people could play against the cover two. Once we got to the red area, opponents had to throw that ball—but we weren't going to give them that much time to do it.

While the Bills gained 166 yards on the ground, they only managed to get 205 passing yards. Kelly completed just 18-of-30 passes and we came away with a 20–19 win.

Belichick's game plan from our Super Bowl victory now resides in the Pro Football Hall of Fame.

He left the Giants to become the Browns' head coach in 1991 and he coached there until he got fired following the 1995 season, just before they became the Baltimore Ravens. Talk about a bad decision for the Browns.

Belichick rejoined Parcells with the Patriots and then the Jets. That led to a bizarre occurrence in 1999 after Parcells decided to step down as the Jets' head coach. Belichick had been earmarked to be the guy to succeed Parcells. But on the day the team introduced him as such to the media, he surprised everyone by resigning. I heard that he wrote a resignation letter on a piece of loose-leaf paper prior to stepping onto the podium. According to reports, the letter said: "I resign as HC of the NYJ."

That proved to be a feeding frenzy for the New York media, particularly when he took the Patriots job shortly thereafter. The Patriots ended up having to surrender a first-round draft pick to the Jets in 2000 for their hiring of Belichick. That might be the best draft choice in NFL history—certainly the best one the Patriots ever made. As luck would have it for the Patriots, they got a first-round-type selection in the sixth round of that draft. Ever heard of a fellow named Tom Brady?

In Belichick's first season, the Patriots failed to make the playoffs after going 5–11. To date, that is his only losing season during his tenure as head coach. In 2001 the Patriots won their first of four Super Bowls under Belichick, who also led the team to two other Super Bowl appearances. Ironically, both of those losses came at the hands of the Giants.

Harry Carson said of Belichick: "We were skeptics initially, but he won us over and we bought into the system. As I listen to what the Patriots are saying, I say that's from the playbook of Belichick and Bill Parcells. It's about team. Don't say anything to make people angry. Don't give anybody anything to write about."

Belichick later credited a lot of his success to his experience coaching with the Giants and winning two Super Bowls. As he told ESPN.com, "It definitely helps to be in a big game and to have won them. You learn something every day, every game. Each year is a learning year, it is a long process. But having done it, then when you go, like to go to the Super Bowl in '01, having been there on a short week like we did, that was a short week, we went on a short week after the San Francisco game, you are not going in there blind."

He added that he knew what he was dealing with.

"I think that helps," he said. "And if you can convey that confidence to everybody else, look, I've been there, I know what we need to do, then maybe that comforts them a little bit. So there certainly is a lot of benefit to it."

Prior to his Patriots facing the Giants in Super Bowl XLVI, Belichick talked glowingly about his "awesome" days with the Giants.

"It was a great job," Belichick said. "It was awesome. I loved that job. I loved coaching the Giants defense. Being in New York, being a part of that great organization and those great players I had the opportunity to coach.

"In all honesty, I wasn't thinking then about if this was what I was going to do at some other point. We were trying to win there. We won in 1986, and it was a great year. We rebuilt the team, and we won again. I was consumed with that. I really just try to live in the moment."

He talked about the great staff the Giants had and the players.

"One of the biggest things I learned, that I can't do today, but I know, is how tough those players were," Belichick said. "We practiced every day in pads—every single day in pads. There were years that we practiced every single day on the turf before we had the grass practice fields up there on the hill. We did 9-on-7—which is a good-tempo running drill—on a regular basis. In training camp, we went out in pads every day. We hit every day. We did 9-on-7 every day. There was no way Bill [Parcells] would go out on the field without doing 9-on-7. We'd skip stretching before we'd skip 9-on-7."

Belichick stressed that the best thing he learned from his days with the Giants was that really good football players had one common element: toughness.

"When you get those guys crashing into each other—Jumbo [Elliott] and Mark Bavaro blocking [Lawrence] Taylor, [Carl] Banks, [Jim] Burt, and all them—they just lined up and played football," Belichick said. "I know it was a different era, but it will never be like that again. I learned players can be tough, they can be physical, they can do more than they think they can do."

THE 3–4 DEFENSE

Not every team can play a 3–4 defense, the defense we played on the Giants.

You've got to have the right personnel. We were very fortunate that we played a defense for which we had exactly the right personnel—the right type of players. We had an organizational philosophy and the Giants tried to draft players to fit that philosophy. We also had the right coaches to run a 3–4.

If you have four good linebackers—and we did have four good linebackers on the Giants every year I played—the 3–4 defense is perfect. I think that it gives you the maximum speed you can have on defense and it gives you a lot of power.

You have a lot of options when you run a 3–4 and you have excellent linebackers. If you have an outside 'backer like me who could bring it off the end, or who could slide to the inside, bring it to the inside, hey, it's a hell of a defense.

The 3–4 has three down linemen—two defensive ends and a nose tackle. Their jobs aren't easy since they're outmanned by the number of guys on the offensive line. Basically what they're trying to do is neutralize the offensive line, or tie them up, which effectively creates opportunities for the four linebackers by allowing them to remain flexible.

Normally it works like this: your nose tackle covers the center. You have two defensive tackles covering the tackles. The inside linebackers cover the guards. We have two outside 'backers. One has the tight end and one is in open space.

Another benefit of the 3–4 is the way it allows a defense to disguise coverages and assignments. If you can give a look that the quarterback or offensive coordinator can't quite figure out, you're all the better off.

For example, you can assign one linebacker to shadow a running back or the quarterback. You can blitz any number from four to zero linebackers on any given play depending on what the situation calls for. Sometimes a linebacker might drop back into pass coverage, and you send the defense back on a blitz, or a "zone blitz." Depending on the offense, one of the linebackers is going to rush.

Basically, all teams either run the 3–4 or they run a 4–3, though now some teams are using a hybrid scheme. A big difference between the two is the play of the nose tackle. In a 3–4, he's got to be a rock. He's a guy that's bigger than your normal defensive lineman because he has to have the strength and the know-how to take care of two gaps while getting double- and triple-teamed a lot of times. If you have a good nose tackle, he'll take a beating, but he gives a beating, too, and he's quick and strong.

Again, we had great linebackers the whole time I was with the Giants, which was a necessity because linebackers in the 3–4 must be more flexible and they have to be better athletes with good size. Sometimes they have to rush the passer and other times they have to act like a defensive lineman by stuffing the running lanes.

This alignment doesn't really affect the defensive backfield. You still have two cornerbacks and two safeties, but it's important that the strong safety is the kind of guy who can line up in the box from time to time to rush the passer. They do their own thing. But the linemen and the linebackers have to be coordinated and on the same page.

I suppose every defense had its heyday at one point or another depending on what the offenses were doing. It's my understanding that the 3–4 really started showing up in defensive systems in the late

1970s. After a while, offenses adjusted to the 3–4 and other defenses came along, putting the 3–4 out to pasture. But it's returned. A lot of NFL teams use the 3–4 these days.

Legendary Oklahoma coach Bud Wilkinson is believed to be the first to use the 3–4 back in the 1940s. When the Dolphins used it in 1972, they became the first team that ran the defense to win a Super Bowl. The Bucs played a good 3–4 defense. It didn't hurt that they had Lee Roy Selmon as one of their down linemen and they had a quality group of linebackers, too. Even though the defense disappeared from the scene for a while after I retired, the Steelers continued to play it. They didn't actually begin running it until 1982, after L.C. Greenwood and Joe Greene retired. They've been playing it ever since.

Having a guy like Brian Kelley calling the signals also helped us run the 3–4. It wasn't that he put me in the best positions. I mean, the defense is called. And I know what the tackle is doing. I know what the nose is doing. I know what the corners are doing. I know what the inside 'backers are doing. So any defensive call, I know where everybody is supposed to be. But playing behind me I had Brian Kelley and Harry Carson. They would tell me, "You can do your thing. We'll back you up."

That meant I didn't have to worry about whether I was going inside or outside. Because even I didn't know which way I would attack until the play began to unfold. And they were smart enough to know that if I'm inside, they should be outside. If I made a mistake, they were there to back me up. I really didn't worry about knowing my assignments, because I knew I could just cause hell with the peace of mind knowing I had two guys behind me who were going to clean it up. That was pretty liberating. I didn't even have to look at a scouting report. It was great. I just went out there like, "I'm going to do what I do and if I mess up, they're going to clean it up."

Even though I say I didn't have to know the other guys' assignments, I did. That was because of Bill Parcells. I had never had a coach that had us know what every player was going to be doing on every play. We'd get tested and would have to go to the blackboard to show what certain players were doing on any given play. I could gamble more because I knew what every position was doing on the football field. I knew what their assignment was. I knew where the safety was going, the tackle. Knowing what they were doing told me what my parameters were. So everybody says, "You did your own thing," but I did it knowing what everybody else was doing.

Since the NFL is now all about the pass, the 3–4 is probably the best defense to use—it's easier to defend the pass since you have four linebackers who can drop back to cover instead of three. On top of that, you can choose to use any combination of linebackers and defensive linemen to rush.

I just think the biggest advantage of the 3–4 compared to the 4–3 is the flexibility it gives you. Even when the play is about to begin from a basic 3–4, one of the linebackers can jump to the front and become a down lineman.

I'm definitely sold on the 3–4.

TRASH TALKING AND INTIMIDATION

There's trash talking and then there's the truth.

Some players think trash talking will intimidate their opponent, the idea being if you talk trash, you must be some kind of badass. I suppose that works in their minds, but the truth is, if you're bringing the trash, you better bring some game.

I never talked that much trash. Why? For starters, I didn't have to talk trash to intimidate the players I played against. I didn't have to talk trash to motivate myself either.

Cheap shots were never a part of my game. To me, the perfect sack was a blind-side shot to the ribs. Once the quarterback rolled over, I wanted to see a snot bubble coming out of his nose. A player remembers it when you put that kind of lick on him, or if you make an athletic play. Trash talking just means you have a big mouth.

When I went on the football field, I wanted you to know that I planned to kick your ass all day—all day! And that was important for me as a player. Once the guy I was going against resigned himself to the fact that there was nothing he could do but struggle to hold his own, he would be toast. I wanted the offensive line to know that there wasn't anything they could do to prevent me from kicking his ass. Knowing that another player is going to kick your ass the length of the football game makes for a tough afternoon for any player.

For sure, that's the way it was for me the first eight or nine years that I played in the league. Adding to the aura I had were all the media reports about how no linebacker had ever terrorized quarterbacks like me and also how I changed the game—how teams couldn't block me with an offensive tackle, so they put a running back on me, too. Still, nobody stopped me. I'm not saying I wasn't getting the job done or that I didn't earn my reputation; I was the guy they were writing and reporting about. I helped perpetuate my reputation for the simple fact that the more you intimidated your opponent, the better off you were. Once O.J. Simpson asked me during an interview about sacking the quarterback and I told him, "You don't want to knock the guy out cold. You want him to be semiconscious and quivering so he can feel it."‘

Mostly I just had fun out there when I played. I mean, the game comes down to this: you've got to hit, you've got to run, and you've got to catch. Football is a brutally physical game and it's not a game for the weak of heart or the weak of mind. But at the end of the day, you still want to play clean football, too.

Opposing players might have been intimidated by me, but they also knew I played the game the right way. In my mind there's no place in the game for dirty football players. I don't like leg whipping and all that stuff. That's dirty football.

Most of the guys I respect to this day were guys who could play hard-nosed football and play it clean.

Sometimes I think about it and I say to myself that I played tough football. I played hard-nosed football, too. But at the end of the day, nobody could say I played dirty football or that I was a dirty player. You knew who the dirty players were. You also knew the guys who just strapped it up and played hard-nosed football. There were a lot of great guys who played that way: Mike Singletary and guys like that that played hard-nosed football and you'll never hear anybody say they were dirty players.

I didn't really get into a whole lot of skirmishes. I might have gotten into some pushing, but that's part of the game.

I respect a lot of players I played with or against, guys such as Joe Montana, Jerry Rice, and Richard Dent. I have respect for a lot of different people for the way they played the game. Take Charles Haley. He was a nut case. But I respect him because he played the game hard. There were so many guys from my era that I respected because I knew they were going to bring it every Sunday.

Basically, I think intimidation is just reputation. The guys I played against were intimidated way before I stepped onto the football field. I built up a reputation and that way, as I got older, I didn't have to do as much as I had to do in the beginning. It's just about intimidating people and living by the reputation you have. Trash talking won't get you that kind of reputation.

BLITZING

Nothing gets a defense going—or the fans going—like blitzing the quarterback and crushing him.

I made a living out of doing that.

The simple explanation of a blitz is more players than normal are sent in to rush the quarterback to try and pressure him into making a bad decision in terms of where he throws the ball. Basically, all hell breaks loose.

On pass plays, five guys are usually blocking—both tackles, both guards, and the center. Obviously, the quarterback is the guy throwing the pass, so he's not blocking. Given that there are 11 offensive players on the field, that means the offense has at least five other options to block on the play, but at least one of the players will be a receiver—and probably more than that. The offense will vary how many guys they call on to pass block based on how much hell the defense is causing. Good quarterbacks have the ability to audible to the right formation if they see the blitz coming.

In theory, the entire defense could blitz on any given play, but that would leave a receiver open if the quarterback could get the pass off in time. It's not a blitz if the defense rushes fewer than five players.

The risky part of a blitz comes in the defense banking on the guys who aren't blitzing being able to cover the guys going out for passes. The idea is to try and create so much havoc that the quarterback won't have time to find the open receiver, so he hurries his throw or takes the sack. For the Giants, that often left the guys playing behind in man coverage because we were getting after the quarterback. If you're trying to blitz and you don't have good cornerbacks and safeties, you might be in trouble. We had both with the Giants.

Blitzing from the 3–4 defense requires having linebackers capable of playing the run who can also drop back into pass coverage.

Fortunately for me, a lot of times when I blitzed I had other guys covering for me.

I don't think there's anything that can turn a game more than a successful blitz. Bringing the heat puts the offense on edge. The quarterback knows if he doesn't read the coverage quickly, he's going to end up on his ass.

There are a lot of different kinds of blitzes. The strong-side stunt blitz is one of the best for stopping the pass—and the run. When you run this, the outside linebacker and defensive end will trade places. That's called a "twist" or a "stunt," and when it's done the right way it can be particularly effective because it confuses the pass blockers. You don't normally run any stunts if you're not expecting a pass because it leaves the defense more vulnerable.

There are two types of commonly used stunts.

In the first type, one of the down linemen will drop back instead of rushing and a linebacker or defensive back will try to burst forward through the spot he left.

The other type involves cross-rushing, in which the linemen change paths for rushing. One or the other might loop around the other player before rushing. The other player could pause momentarily, too, waiting until the player he switches with penetrates a little bit before cutting through the space created by that charge.

A lot of times our defensive end would shoot the "C gap," then I'd rush off his backside and charge through the "B gap" toward the quarterback. The gaps between the center and either guard is called the "A gap," the gaps between the guards and tackles are called the

"B gap," and outside of both tackles is the "C gap." Sometimes the inside linebacker on the strong side—the side where the tight end is lined up—will focus on the offensive guard and delay blitz through the A gap.

When you hear about "backside pressure," it's all about the nose tackle shooting through the A gap on the back side or the side where the action isn't headed. That allows the weak-side defensive end to rush the B gap. If I didn't have the freedom I had with my fellow linebackers, I would have been held responsible for the outside rush lane and the area out in the flat for pass coverage.

Of course, there are all kinds of games within the game when it comes to blitzing. For example, if the offense has a tight end who excels at blocking, he can take out a stunt. That allows the offense a chance to hurt you with a sweep.

You can also do all kinds of things to try and confuse the quarterback by sending an inside linebacker through the B gap, then having the outside linebacker go through the A gap.

A really good offensive line communicates well. They can sniff out a blitz before the ball is snapped and they call blocking signals to try and patch where they figure the hole is going to be created so the dam doesn't break. Of course, the quarterback can audible too.

The bottom line on blitzing is it usually comes down to whether the quarterback can get a quick read and get the ball off before the heat arrives. Fortunately, when I played for the Giants we were pretty good at winning that battle.

RAY PERKINS

Rays Perkins coached the Giants when I first arrived. He never really said a lot to me and he didn't show a lot of emotion, but I never had a problem with that. The way he looked at you, you were never sure if you wanted to say hello or not. I think Ray understood I had the talent. And I think he's the one who gave Bill Parcells the ok to let me freelance a little bit. Coach Perkins definitely knew talent. He knew discipline, too. He also understood the allure of New York's nightlife.

He became the head coach of the Giants in 1979. When he arrived, it was like a new sheriff was in town. I hear a lot of stories about when he first started coaching the team.

For instance, one year in training camp during a team meeting everybody was grumbling about how hard the practices were. Some of the veterans decided to take the gripe to Perkins, like they were going to revolt if the practices didn't get easier. Perkins told them he didn't care if all of them left.

Brian Kelley used to tell a story about a live scrimmage that took place after a Saturday-night game. That pissed everybody off. After learning his team was unhappy about the scrimmage, he said he didn't really give a damn. And, according to Brian, he added: "I'll play with 22 fucking rookies."

Perkins was born and raised in Mississippi before he attended the University of Alabama. He was a wide receiver for the Crimson Tide when they won national championships in 1964 and 1965 under the guidance of legendary coach Bear Bryant. Future Hall of Fame quarterback Joe Namath and Perkins had even been teammates. He earned All-American honors his senior season in 1966.

Perkins played for Don Shula on the Baltimore Colts for four seasons. He was on the Colts when they lost to Namath's Jets in the third Super Bowl, which is still considered the biggest upset in pro football history. Probably his biggest play in the NFL came when Johnny Unitas tossed him a 68-yard touchdown in the 1970 AFC Championship Game against the Raiders. That sparked a 27–17 Colts win and earned the Colts a spot in Super Bowl V.

After his playing days were over, Perkins worked as an assistant coach for the New England Patriots and San Diego Chargers before landing his first head coaching job with the Giants. He left the Giants at the conclusion of the 1982 season to take over at Alabama for Bryant after Bryant retired.

We'd won three in a row and looked like we were headed for the playoffs when Perkins broke the news that he'd be leaving us to take the Alabama job. We then dropped two in a row and we were basically out of it, even though it took the final Sunday of the season to determine that.

Alabama is one of the best jobs around. Nobody could get mad at him for leaving the Giants and going back to his alma mater to coach. One thing about Perkins, he was an honest guy and he always seemed to be upfront. Everybody on the team knew that if the Alabama job ever opened up he'd likely take it if it were offered to him. That job was one of his main goals, so who can be mad at a guy for going after his dream?

That looked to me like a tough deal to get into, though. Bryant had been there for so many years and had become such a legend that the guy to follow him couldn't possibly fill his shoes. Even though Perkins wanted to take the job, a lot of people thought he was wading into a no-win situation.

It's always a tough situation to follow somebody who is a legend. Take Ray Handley; he had to handle a tough situation, too, when he followed Bill Parcells as the head coach of the Giants. Losing Parcells was probably one of the biggest tragedies to ever happen to the Giants. Of course, Parcells got the job after Perkins left.

Perkins coached at Alabama from 1983 through 1986 and his teams went 32–15–1 and won three bowl games. Predictably, the alumni did not like him, so he left after four years when he got a nice offer to coach the Tampa Bay Buccaneers. Getting away from Alabama probably was a good move, even though he didn't do anything with the Bucs. I'm not sure anybody's ever really replaced Bear Bryant at Alabama, though Nick Saban has done a hell of a job. He's done such a good job that the guy who eventually replaces him is going to go through the same thing Perkins did at Alabama.

Perkins never won a Super Bowl with the Giants. In fact, he had three losing seasons and one playoff berth. But the bottom line is this: he helped change the culture of a losing franchise.

Perkins coached the Bucs from 1987 to 1990 before getting fired midway through the 1990 season, leaving him with a 42–75 career coaching mark in the NFL. He then coached a year at Arkansas State University in 1992 before taking the offensive coordinator job for the Patriots under Parcells. He stayed in that job until 1997, when he moved west to take the same position with the Oakland Raiders.

He finished out his coaching career at Jones County Junior College in Ellisville, Mississippi, where he resigned after the 2013 season.

Thanksgiving Day
Touchdown

S acks were my thing, not touchdowns.

I only scored three touchdowns during my career. All of them came on passes I intercepted and returned for six points. Some of that probably had to do with the fact that I rushed the passer a lot more than I dropped back into pass coverage.

Of those, the touchdown I scored in 1982 against the Lions on national TV is probably the one people remember most.

The 1982 season brought the 63rd regular season of the NFL and a 57-day players' strike. That reduced the season from 16 games to nine, and the NFL implemented a 16-team playoff tournament. That whole season felt like a weird deal.

We were 0–3 heading into our Thanksgiving Day game against the Lions in Pontiac, Michigan. They were 2–1. Both teams were playing their second game in the eight days since the strike had ended. We were 0–2 prior to the strike and 0–1 afterward. Obviously, with only six games left in the season, we knew we'd better get something going or we weren't going to the postseason.

Thanksgiving Day games have been a regular NFL occurrence since the league began in 1920. These days there are three NFL games played on Thanksgiving. The Detroit Lions and the Dallas Cowboys host two of them on a regular basis and a third game, with random opponents, has been played annually since 2006. Everybody wanted to play in those Thanksgiving Day games because they were nationally televised. We only played twice on Thanksgiving during my career, and that 1982 game became the first of those two games.

I went into that game in a bad mood. Because I had a sore knee, I didn't start for the first time in my career. I still ended up playing, though. Despite my injury, I felt like I could run, and that proved to be true.

That game turned out to be a sloppy one.

Scott Brunner started at quarterback for us and he threw a couple of interceptions, both of which led to field goals by Eddie Murray.

The Lions started Eric Hipple at quarterback and he'd been totally ineffective in the first half, so they brought in Gary Danielson to start the second half.

Harry Carson intercepted one of Danielson's passes at the start of the third quarter to cue up a field goal by Joe Danelo. I managed to get a good shot at their running back, Billy Sims, on the Lions' next possession, and he fumbled. Brad Van Pelt recovered for us to set up another Danelo field goal to tie the game at 6.

Based on the fact only 12 points had been scored in the first three quarters, you just knew a lot of people had already wolfed down their Thanksgiving meals and checked out of our game to retreat to their pillows for afternoon naps.

We had 11 minutes left to play in the fourth quarter when Danielson led a drive that put the Lions at our 3-yard line facing third-and-goal.

They called a timeout. When they returned and lined up for their play, I recognized the formation as one similar to what the Packers had used in our second game of the season. That told me to look for a pass play. I needed to cover the man coming out of the backfield when he went out into the flat.

Danielson dropped back to pass and threw the ball out to his left toward the sideline, hoping to connect with Horace King, who went into the flat as expected. I cut in front of him and got the pass. I had nothing but green in front of me and I had a full head of steam.

Since I could run a little bit back then, I took that one the distance. My knee didn't bother me at all on the return, which covered 97 yards and gave us a 13–7 lead. All I could see on the play was our coach, Ray Perkins, going crazy. He was waving his arms and yelling for me to "keep going."

I thought I'd get caught when I saw a shadow. I figured it was a Lions player chasing me. Turned out it was my own shadow.

I slid into the end zone when I got there and was greeted by our cornerback, Terry Jackson, who had run down the sideline with me. A flag got thrown on the play and everybody thought the touchdown would get taken off the board, but it turned out to be offensive pass interference and the play stood.

Danielson brought the Lions back down the field later in the game, but Jackson intercepted the ball nearly at the same spot I'd made my interception and we had our first win of the season.

Sims ran for 114 yards on 26 carries against us that day. He could play. That was only the second time in 21 games at that point that the other team had a running back gain 100 yards against us. Despite Sims' performance, Coach Perkins told us after the game that we had played like the Giants from the previous year and that we needed to continue to do so in our final five games if we wanted to have any shot at making the playoffs.

We followed with wins against the Houston Oilers and the Eagles before losing two of our final three games to finish at 4–5 and out of the playoffs.

GEORGE YOUNG

George Young put the Giants together. He was the brains behind the brains on the field. I respected George Young. I think he had a great football mind.

Young, who died in 2001, made the decisions that turned around the franchise and fueled Super Bowl appearances—and wins—in 1986 and 1991. But he did more than just win two Super Bowls. He built an organization by drafting the right people and making the right hires.

Young was born in Baltimore, where he became a standout at Calvert Hall College High School as a baseball and football player. He went on to attend Bucknell and started at defensive tackle for three seasons, serving as a team captain for Bucknell's undefeated 1951 team. In addition, he earned Little All-America and All-East first-team honors his senior season. The Dallas Texans (the team that became the Baltimore Colts) selected him in the 26th round of the 1952 draft. After getting cut by the Texans in final cuts, he went home to Baltimore to take a junior high teaching job. Three teams tried to sign him the following year, but he'd already made up his mind that he wanted to teach history and political science and coach high school football. He went on to win six state titles during his 15 years of coaching high school football for Calvert Hall, then City College High.

Along the way, he earned master's degrees from Johns Hopkins and Loyola. He also met Colts coach Don Shula, who recognized a football mind when he saw one. In 1967, Shula hired Young as a consultant, scout, and then offensive line coach and coordinator. Young later became an assistant coach under Shula when Shula took the job as the Dolphins' head coach.

After the Giants fired coach John McVay and Andy Robustelli resigned as the Giants' director of football operations, Wellington Mara and Tim Mara, the co-owners of the Giants, had different ideas about who could lead the team. That's when NFL commissioner Pete Rozelle advised them to hire Young in 1979. They did, and Young hung his neck out almost immediately, showing that he wasn't afraid to make a call—even if it wasn't the popular one.

In Young's first draft in 1979 he had not even been the Giants' general manager for three months, and he elected to use the seventh overall pick to take an unknown quarterback from Morehead State: Phil Simms.

George's philosophy was to always hire people you knew so you had a good idea about what the person was like, with no surprises. He was the same way with talent. Prior to the draft he'd sent his head coach, Ray Perkins, to work out Simms. The Giants and Young got heavily criticized for drafting Simms, though time proved him right. He would later explain that he always felt that a person should "assert" himself, adding: "You just can't be reacting to what people think you should do. You don't often wind up with a great arm and the intelligence to go with it. It's the kind of opportunity that might not occur for another two years. When you get it, you've got to take it."

Another big call for Young came when Perkins left the team to take the job at Alabama after the 1982 season. Young decided to hire a young assistant. That guy's name was Bill Parcells. Simms and Parcells—two pretty strong calls, right?

Other strong calls by Young include drafting me, though the Giants had the No. 2 pick, so it was going to either be me or running back George Rogers, whom the Saints took with the No. 1 pick.

Trading for Ottis Anderson was a biggie, too. He didn't draft Ottis out of the University of Miami when he had the chance in 1979 because he went with Simms. But he did trade two draft picks for him in 1986, and that proved to be a solid move—particularly in Super Bowl XXV when Ottis won MVP honors in our victory over Buffalo.

Wellington Mara told the *New York Daily News* that Young's success had to be measured more in terms of the organization he built and the people he brought in to build it. Young's draft picks brought 23 Pro Bowlers into the organization during his tenure that extended through the 1997 season, a period that saw the Giants go 155–139–2. He was named the NFL's executive of the year five times.

Paul Tagliabue reigned as the NFL commissioner when George died, and he said of him: "He was the quintessential 'football guy' who had the unique ability to be at home in the locker room, boardroom or any room in his beloved Baltimore....He was in essence a teacher, both in the history class and in football, who helped people at all levels. No one cared more about the game of football than George Young. He loved it and lived it for his entire life. His contributions place him in rare company with the legends of the game."

Young wasn't afraid to get into it with any of his coaches when they wanted to make changes he did not want to make. But it worked.

In addition to winning two Super Bowls under his watch, the Giants also won four NFC East titles before he left in 1997 to work for Tagliabue as a senior vice president of football operations for the NFL.

DISMAL 1983 SEASON

I've never enjoyed losing, whether it's on the golf course, in darts, anything. I especially didn't like losing when I played football. Fortunately, I only experienced four losing seasons during my 13 NFL seasons.

The first one came in 1982, which was a crazy year because of the strike. We finished that reduced season with a 4–5 mark. While I wasn't happy about that, the following season is the one that never has sat well with me. I've never forgotten that one. We went 3–12–1 that year. And we had good players, I thought. We just couldn't win games.

I went into that season feeling pretty good about the fact that Bill Parcells had been named the team's head coach after Rays Perkins left for Alabama. I'd felt close to Bill since my rookie season in 1981 and had him as my defensive coordinator. I thought he deserved the chance to be the head guy, and a lot of other guys were happy, too.

We began that season 1–2 before we hosted the Packers at Giants Stadium and came away with a 27–3 win. After that I felt that we had righted the ship. I figured in the two consecutive home games after we played the Packers we would be able to get on a roll that would take us to the playoffs. Boy did I read that one wrong.

The first of those home games came against the San Diego Chargers, who had the great Dan Fouts at quarterback. The man liked to throw the football and he tossed two touchdown passes in the first half before having to leave the game in the third quarter with a shoulder injury. Meanwhile, we'd erased a 17-point first-half lead and they had their second-string quarterback, Ed Luther, running their offense.

Turns out, that didn't matter.

Luther hit a big 32-yard pass to Charlie Joyner that took the Chargers to our 45 late in the fourth quarter. Then we got a steady diet of Chuck Muncie on three consecutive players. On the last of those he ran 34 yards around left end to give them a 41–34 win.

Our season went south from there.

After that we went on an 0–6–1 stretch before we finally won again by beating the Eagles 23–0 at Philadelphia. Then we lost our next three games to move to 3–11–1 heading into our last game of the season against the Redskins.

There's nothing worse than losing, man. And one thing I learned about losing is that losing seems to breed more losing. That season we seemed to find ways to lose games instead of winning them. So the way we finished brought a suitable end to the frustration.

We traveled to Washington, D.C., to play the Redskins at RFK Stadium. They were 13–2 and needed to win to ensure an NFC East title. But we led 12–7 at halftime. We improved our chances to win in the third quarter when Joe Morris caught a six-yard touchdown from Jeff Rutledge to put us up 19–7.

Two true things: losing teams find a way to lose and winning teams find a way to win. And that's exactly what happened.

Joe Theismann wasn't having his best day early in the game. We picked off three of his passes in the first quarter and grabbed another later in the game. Still, he found a way to get their offense on track.

Before the third quarter was over, he ran one in from three yards out to cut the lead to 19–14. They added a field goal, but we answered with three points to put us up 22–17 after Ali Haji-Sheikh hit from 28 yards. That gave Haji-Sheikh five field goals for the game and established a season record with 35 for the season (that has since been broken). That would be it for our offense.

Theismann added a seven-yard touchdown pass and John Riggins bulled in from two yards out for their final score to give them a 31–22 win. That was embarrassing. We finished the season at 3–12–1. Can you imagine only winning three games in a season? And we'd won just seven times in two seasons.

It was hard for me to enjoy anything when we were losing like we were.

Earlier that season, I'd reached the end of my rope after our 20–20 overtime tie with the St. Louis Cardinals. I actually thought about quitting. The kind of football we were playing just pissed me off. Finally, I talked to Parcells for about two hours and he convinced me better days were ahead for us.

What added to the frustration was the fact we had some pretty good players. We just didn't have the attitude we needed to win. We needed to have more pride than what we had, and we needed a few more players.

After a season like that, we wondered if Parcells' job was at risk, too. Fortunately, he remained in place as the team's coach, which is probably the best thing that ever happened to the franchise. Sometimes the best moves are the ones that aren't made.

Our fortunes began to turn around after that season, but I still remember how frustrated I was during that 1983 season.

BEARS LESSON

We thought we were a Super Bowl contender when we played the Chicago Bears in the playoffs in 1986. Instead, that game taught us a lesson about where we had to get to in order to become that team.

The 1985 season went well for us. We finished with a 10–6 record, which was good for second place in the NFC East and earned us a Wild Card spot in the playoffs. We beat the defending Super Bowl Champion San Francisco 49ers in the first round. Since they'd beaten us in the playoffs the previous season, we were feeling pretty good about ourselves. We had momentum and we knew we were going to need it playing the Bears.

The "Monsters of the Midway" had only lost one game during the regular season and were set as 8½-point favorites over us. They had a tenacious defense known as the 46 defense that was masterminded by their defensive coach, Buddy Ryan, and the game would be played at their place, Soldier Field in Chicago.

Figuring out their overall team philosophy didn't take a genius. From the opening snap they tried to intimidate the teams they played on both sides of the ball. I always felt like the toughest team won most of the time. So I felt pretty good about our chances despite the success the Bears had enjoyed that season.

Leading up to the game we heard plenty of talk from the Bears.

And we were pretty vocal, too.

The Bears had finished the season ranked as the NFL's top defense. Ryan's 46 defense certainly had lived up to its billing. They'd line up six guys on the line and get after the quarterback. If that wasn't intimidating enough, they ran all sorts of blitz variations in that defense.

Middle linebacker Mike Singletary led that defense. He led them in tackles and earned NFL Defensive Player of the Year honors. Flanking him on the outside were Wilbur Marshall and Otis Wilson, who had six and 10.5 sacks, respectively.

Hard to believe there were any sacks left to be had with that defensive line they had. Defensive end Richard Dent led the NFL with 17 sacks; Dan Hampton, the end on the other side, had 6.5 sacks; the interior of the line had defensive tackle Steve McMichael, who had eight sacks; and 350-pound William "The Refrigerator" Perry tallied five sacks.

The pressure those guys caused helped their starting defensive backfield come up with 20 interceptions.

That's one of the best defenses ever.

Of course we were pretty good, too. We were ranked as the second-best defensive team that season. That didn't mean much to the Bears, though. Wilson got quoted as saying, "There's no comparison" when he was asked to compare our defense to theirs. "They're only talking about one linebacker. What's his name?" Of course he was talking about me. He finished his comment by saying, "I think we should be talked about more."

On offense we had Phil Simms at quarterback, and he'd had a good season throwing for 3,829 yards and 22 touchdowns. We also had Joe Morris at running back. He didn't have a lot of size at 5'7", 195 pounds, but he ran hard and gained 1,336 yards while scoring 21 touchdowns in 1985. They knew they'd have to stop Joe. Yet that prospect didn't seem to concern Wilson either. He noted: "We're the best at stopping the run, so I don't see a problem."

Ryan did not lack confidence in his defense: "I don't think any team in the NFL is ready for us right now. A week isn't enough for the Giants or any other team to prepare for our defense."

Carl Banks countered for us by saying, "We're not going to let anybody walk on the field with a reputation and take it away from us."

And Gary Reasons said the Bears "can be had, believe me."

Chicago running back Matt Suhey might have expressed the only morsel of truth uttered by either team that week when he said: "A lot of guys are scared to death that we're going to lose. We've played so well for so long, and now if we lose, the season's gone."

While everybody talked about the Bears defense, they had a pretty nice offense led by their quarterback, Jim McMahon. Cocky son of a bitch, that McMahon, and he brought a different challenge to our defense than what we'd had the week before when facing the 49ers and Joe Montana.

Montana was a mobile quarterback, but we knew he wasn't too effective when he scrambled to his left. We were able to force him to scramble to his left and that made him less likely to succeed.

We had our right defensive end pinch Montana back toward the middle. Our defensive coordinator, Bill Belichick, substituted Andy Headen for Gary Reasons at linebacker on passing downs. Normally Headen would be my backup—he could move a little better than Gary so that helped us keep Montana from getting outside the pocket and put our nose tackle, Jim Burt, in position to make the sack. He had two of our four sacks on the day.

With McMahon, we knew he felt comfortable heading either direction out of the pocket. We were facing a guy who was more active than Montana. He might not have been as good of a passer as Montana, but the dude could scramble and improvise. That made him more dangerous than Montana. He could be explosive, too. Everybody had seen the Bears' nationally televised game when he came off the bench to throw three touchdowns in seven minutes to lead the team to a 33–24 win over the Vikings.

McMahon was a tough guy and a leader, too. He certainly wasn't afraid of leaving the pocket.

The Bears also had Walter Payton in their backfield. Despite the 1985 season being his 11th in the league, he rushed for 1,551 yards and led the team with 49 catches. Payton could hit the line hard and was a bruising runner. You paid the price when you tackled him. Once he got through the line, he had great speed. He could break a long one at any time.

The media asked Bill Parcells how he planned to stop Payton. Our head coach responded: "Jeeps, ropes, a lasso."

We'd been to the playoffs three times to that point and won the Wild Card game each time. We knew we had to take the next step. We had to beat the best and the Bears were the best, even if we'd already beaten the defending Super Bowl champions in the first week of the playoffs.

Soldier Field hosted its first postseason game since 1963 and the weather responded with classic Chicago conditions. Kickoff came at 11:30 AM and we played in 18 degrees with a minus-12 wind-chill factor. Nobody should ever claim the weather as a cause for winning or losing, but it definitely played a factor in our poor start.

Sean Landeta came on to punt early in the first quarter and when he tried to get his foot on the ball, he just barely nipped it. I'd never seen anything like that, but the wind had affected the drop to his foot. Shaun Gayle picked up the ball at our 5 and strolled into the end zone to put the Bears up 7–0.

Landeta said of his nightmare: "The wind just blew it. I did everything normal, but when I dropped the ball, I saw it moving....The wind would come up and then let down. It was moving the ball on my drops some during warmups and I hoped it wouldn't come up when I had to kick during the game....It had never happened before. Never. Not even just messing around on the sidelines. I had never swung and missed. I just thought to myself, 'This is unbelievable.' As soon as I dropped the ball, I knew I wasn't going to get it good. I tried to chase it, but I'm not even sure I got it at all. The first thing I did after that was try to go after the ball, but then I saw them pick it up and run it in. It was just unreal."

You couldn't make any mistakes like that against a team like that Bears team. You were lucky to beat them if you made no mistakes and we had a handful. Landeta's botched punt got them going like blood in the water does a shark.

We held them scoreless for the remainder of the first half. McMahon got something going in the third quarter and hit Dennis McKinnon for a 23-yard touchdown and a 14–0 lead. That might as well have been 42–0 at that point. They weren't making mistakes and they were playing tough, hard-nosed football.

McMahon threw another touchdown pass to McKinnon in the third quarter and that completed the scoring in a 21–0 loss.

If we could have eliminated three or four plays, the game would have been even. We weren't discouraged afterward, though. I felt like we could play with those guys.

Parcells later called that Bears team "one of the best teams I've ever coached against," and allowed that if our 1985 team played them 10 times we might have beaten them two or three times.

That Bears team was better than us. But after that game, we started getting better and better.

Parcells said that game against the Bears "showed me what we have to do to reach their level and, I'll tell you, we're not that far away."

We filed that one away and took Bill's sentiment to heart.

CHAPTER 2

THE BIG GAMES

1987 DIVISIONAL PLAYOFF

January 4, 1987
Giants 49, 49ers 3

Even though we finished the 1986 regular season with a 14–2 record, questions remained about our postseason chances. Could we move through the 49ers in the first round of the playoffs to advance toward the Super Bowl?

We were to host the 49ers in our first playoff game when, just five weeks earlier, we'd somehow managed to take a 21–17 win after falling behind to them during a *Monday Night Football* game.

Even though we managed to rush for just 13 yards in that game, we outscored the 49ers 21–0 in the second half to take the win in San Francisco. The script from that game didn't exactly evoke confidence in Giants nonbelievers, and likely explained why we were just three-point favorites even though we were playing at home. Of course, the Giants weren't exactly known for championships at the time. The last time the franchise had been to a championship game was in 1963 when the Bears defeated the Giants to claim the NFL Championship.

But something flipped for us. We were a different team than the previous time we played the 49ers. Joe Montana and company learned that one the hard way.

Phil Simms connected with Mark Bavaro for a 24-yard touchdown in the first quarter and the 49ers answered with a field goal to make it 7–3 heading into the second quarter. That's when we found another gear.

Joe Morris scored on a 45-yard touchdown run and Simms found Bobby Johnson on a 15-yard touchdown. I got in on the scoring when I picked off a pass and took it 34 yards for a touchdown to give us a 28–3 lead at the half.

Jim Burt hit Montana when he was throwing a pass in the second quarter and Montana had to leave the game with a concussion.

Once the second half began, we continued where we left off, scoring three more touchdowns in the third quarter to give us a 49–3 lead.

Our defense swarmed that day. Both sides of the ball were hungry for us.

Morris only gained 14 yards in 13 carries in our first game against the 49ers. This time around, he banged for 159 yards on 24 carries, scoring two touchdowns.

All told, our offense ran for 216 yards on 44 carries. And remember—that came against a really good defense. They'd only allowed 97.2 yards rushing during the regular season.

Meanwhile, Simms was efficient, completing nine passes in 19 attempts for 136 yards along with four touchdowns.

Quite a day.

Of course, you had to credit our coaching staff for the adjustments they made for going up against the 49ers' defense.

Essentially, they had played an eight-man front in that game, with their strong safety, Carlton Williamson, lined up on the line of scrimmage. Their free safety, Ronnie Lott, would move up to help support their run defense, which allowed Williamson to shift back for pass coverage.

Our coaching staff anticipated correctly. We used an extra tight end in Zeke Mowatt so they couldn't overload the strong side and that kept them guessing. The results were right there on the stats sheet.

Afterward, their coach, the great Bill Walsh, told the media, "They played a perfect game. We were shattered by a great team. I believe they will go all the way."

I think that was our best defensive game that year. We had intensity and we were aggressive. Nobody let up the entire game.

1987 NFC
CHAMPIONSHIP GAME

January 11, 1987
Giants 17, Redskins 0

Winning big can sometimes leave a team flat. We defeated the San Francisco 49ers 49–3 in our first playoff game of 1986 to earn a spot in the NFC Championship Game.

Everything had worked the week before. Could we come through with another solid performance against the Redskins? If that happened, we knew we'd be headed to the Super Bowl for the first time in franchise history.

Giants Stadium swelled with 76,633 screaming fans backing us against a quality Redskins team that could throw the long ball and came into the game averaging 350 yards per game during the season.

The weather favored the defense that day. Winds were gusting over 30 mph, so running the football looked like the ideal game plan. Those conditions certainly didn't favor a team trying to come from behind by throwing the football.

Bill Parcells had studied the field conditions throughout the morning and understood how tough moving the football against the wind was going to be. So he instructed our captain, Harry Carson, to pick having the wind at our back if we won the toss. We won it, and that's what we did.

Fortunately, we were able to grab an early lead.

After we kicked off, we forced the Redskins to punt and their punter, Steve Cox, fell prey to the win, hitting a 23-yard kick that wobbled the whole way and gave us possession at the Redskins' 47.

Joe Morris ran for a first down, which led to Raul Allegre's 47-yard field goal that put us up 3–0.

When the Redskins got the ball back, we stopped them again, and again they punted. This time Cox got off a 27-yard punt and we took over at their 38.

Phil Simms had the wind at his back and completed a huge pass on third-and-20 when he hooked up with Lionel Manuel for 25 yards to move the ball to their 11. That was a big catch for Manuel, too, because he'd been out for most of the season and that was his first catch since our third game.

Simms followed that up by connecting with Bobby Johnson for a touchdown, but it got called back because of a motion penalty. On the next play, Manuel ran a post pattern into double coverage. The Redskins chased Simms out of the pocket and Manuel knew to try and find an open spot, which he did. Simms hit him in the right side of the end zone to give us a 10-point lead.

On the Redskins' next possession, they tried to go to the air. Even with the wind in his face, quarterback Jay Schroeder could fire the football. And he dropped one into Gary Clark's arms after he got behind our secondary. Somehow he couldn't get a handle on that one and the Redskins again had to punt.

In the second quarter, the Redskins finally had the wind at their back. Schroeder could throw the ball as far as he wanted to throw the thing. If the Redskins were going to catch us, we knew the second quarter would be their big chance. That chance came early in the quarter when they drove the ball to our 34. We held them, and they had to try a field goal, but their center botched the snap and we recovered the ball at their 49.

Simms then hit our tight end Mark Bavaro for a 30-yard gain, and Morris capped the drive with a 1-yard touchdown run to give us a 17–0 lead.

The Redskins had one more opportunity to get back in the game in the second quarter when Morris fumbled at our 37. But we stuffed their running back George Rogers on a fourth-and-1 and that seemed to take the wind out of their sails. Here they were falling behind us when they had the wind in their faces, and then they couldn't score when they had the wind behind them.

Our defense did what it had to do all day. The Bears had gone to the Super Bowl and dominated the year before. I remember thinking we looked like the Bears out there that day. The way they played in the playoffs, shutting everyone out, was the way we played that day.

We outgained the Redskins 117-to-40 on the ground and Schroeder only completed 20 passes in 50 attempts. They were 0-for-14 on third-down attempts and gained just 190 yards total on the day.

Giants Stadium went nuts. After all, we were headed to the Super Bowl. But we didn't celebrate the same way. We knew the job was not yet done. We had a Super Bowl to play and the only way we were going to consider that 1986 season a successful one was by winning it all.

Super Bowl XXI

January 25, 1987
Giants 39, Broncos 20

I'd been in the NFL for five years when the 1986 season began, and that one turned out to be something special. We went to the first Super Bowl in team history and we played for the first league championship since the Giants of Y.A. Tittle and Sam Huff lost to the Bears in the 1963 NFL Championship Game.

We had a young, veteran team. Most of us were only in our early-to-mid 20s, but we'd played into January for three straight years. We had that postseason experience.

Our quarterback, Phil Simms, could throw it around a little bit. Just look at his numbers from that season: 3,487 passing yards and 21 touchdowns.

But our offense was balanced and it could be bruising, beginning with one of Simms' favorite targets, tight end Mark Bavaro, who was only 23 years old. "Rambo" caught 66 passes that season for over 1,000 yards, and he could knock you on your ass, too.

We also had a pretty good crop of receivers in Bobby Johnson, Stacy Robinson, and Phil McConkey. And we were a Bill Parcells–coached team, which meant we believed in pounding the football. Most of our ground work fell on Joe Morris' shoulders.

Joe set a then–franchise record that season by rushing for 1,516 yards. He also scored 14 touchdowns and brought toughness to our offense. Our fullback, Maurice Carthon, did a nice job of helping to open holes and we had a great offensive line.

Our defense could handle its side of the ball as well, bringing a nice balance to the team.

I had one of my better seasons in 1986. I led the league in sacks, with 20.5, and I won the NFL Defensive Player of the Year Award for the third time. They also voted me as the winner of the NFL Most Valuable Player Award, making me just the second defensive player to do so. But I had plenty of help from our defense, which earned the nickname "Big Blue Wrecking Crew."

Jim Burt played nose tackle and Leonard Marshall right end. Both of them were Pro Bowl selections. The other starting linebackers were an accomplished group including Harry Carson, Carl Banks, and Gary Reasons.

The Cowboys scored 31 against us in the first game of the season, but we held our next 14 opponents to 20 points or fewer until the last game of the season, when we beat the Packers 55–24.

We finished the regular season at 14–2, and the city was pretty excited about the prospect of having a Super Bowl champion in the same season the New York Mets won the World Series.

The playoffs were more of the same. We rolled, beating the 49ers 49–3 and the Redskins 17–0 to reach the Super Bowl against the Broncos.

John Elway was the star of the Broncos, leading the team to an 11–5 record during the regular season. What made a quarterback like him dangerous were his skills at creating something out of nothing. Being a big, physical quarterback with a powerful arm helped make that happen. You had to respect the ability of a player like that. No surprise that he ended up in the Hall of Fame.

Other than Elway, the Broncos had a solid group of wide receivers with Steve Watson, Mark Jackson, and Vance Johnson and a pretty good tight end in Orson Mobley. So they could spread the ball around pretty well. Sammy Winder and Gerald Willhite were decent running backs, and they had a good offensive line, including a Pro Bowl selection at guard, Keith Bishop. But clearly, Elway was the show. We knew he was the guy we had to stop.

He'd been the difference in the Broncos' playoff wins against the Patriots and Browns. Most remember that 23–20 Broncos win over the Browns because of "The Drive," which saw Elway lead the team on a 98-yard, 15-play drive to tie the game and send it into overtime, where the Broncos won on a Rich Karlis field goal. Like I said, the guy was dangerous.

Because I got after quarterbacks pretty well—and Elway was a really good quarterback—a lot of the pre-game hype centered on Lawrence Taylor versus John Elway.

We beat the Broncos 19–16 in Week 12. Elway threw for more than 300 yards that day, but he also threw two interceptions and they had four turnovers in all. Still, we only beat them by three points.

Since it was my first Super Bowl, I was pretty jacked up. With all the sitting around and waiting for two weeks until you played such a big game, you wouldn't be human if you weren't excited.

Elway got the Broncos off and running with a couple of critical passes on their first drive. Jackson caught a 24-yard pass to give them the ball at our 39, but we were able to hold them after that and they had to settle for a Karlis field goal from 48 yards out to give them a 3–0 lead.

Our offense answered.

Simms finished off a nine-play, 78-yard drive with a six-yard touchdown pass to Zeke Mowatt to give us a 7–3 lead. Then we gave the Broncos a touchdown, and that was partly my fault.

Ken Bell returned the kickoff to their 42 before Elway hit three straight passes. On one of those passes to Winder, the officials called a personal foul on Harry Carson for hitting Winder after he was out of bounds. Then I picked up an unsportsmanlike conduct penalty for picking up the penalty marker on that play and throwing it. That was one of those heat-of-the-moment-type things, and I could have kicked myself afterward for doing something so stupid. That gave them the ball at our 6-yard line and led to an Elway draw for a 4-yard touchdown.

Early in the second quarter, we forced Elway out of the pocket on third down. Somehow, he managed to scramble away and complete a 54-yard pass to Johnson. They moved the ball to our 1-yard line and had the chance to push their lead.

Elway rolled right on the first play and I chased after him, grabbing his shirt and yanking him down around the 2. Carson stopped Gerald Willhite for no gain on the next play, then Carl Banks tackled Winder for a 4-yard loss when they tried to run a sweep. Karlis' 23-yard field goal missed, leaving them empty. I felt like that was a turning point for us, and things got even better before the end of the half.

With less than minutes to play in the first half, George Martin sacked Elway for a 13-yard loss and a safety, so we went into halftime trailing 10–9.

After the intermission, we got things going, scoring four touchdowns and a field goal in our first five possessions of the half. Critical in that run was a play in our first series. Facing a fourth down, Parcells sent in the punt team along with our backup quarterback Jeff Rutledge. He lined up under center with our punter, Sean Landeta, moving out to wide receiver. Rutledge ran an option and picked up two yards for the first down at our 48. That kept alive the drive that led to Simms hooking up with Bavaro on a 13-yard touchdown pass.

The Broncos managed to gain two net yards while running 10 offensive plays in the third quarter. A big part of our defensive success in the second half was a change of philosophy by balancing our pass rush.

We only rushed three guys from one side and one from the other in the first half. Elway recognized what we were doing and flowed to the open area to make plays. Of the passes he completed in the first half there were deep ones of 54, 31, and 24 yards. Something needed to change. So in the second half we sent an equal number of guys from each side. That allowed us to do a better job of keeping him in the pocket. We formed an umbrella and he wasn't able to roll out and hit those big passes. Good thing, because we knew at halftime if we didn't rein him in we were in trouble.

We kept the pedal to the metal until we came away with a 39–20 win.

Our team had plenty of heroes in that game, but nobody could outshine Simms, who was the MVP of the game. At one point he completed 10 consecutive passes on the way to completing an incredible 22 passes in 25 attempts for 268 yards and three touchdowns.

Three incompletions in 25 passes still blows my mind. That's an 88 percent completion rate, good for three touchdowns and 268 yards of offense. It remains the single greatest performance by a quarterback in any Super Bowl.

Simms said of his performance: "I felt we could move the ball on them, but not in my wildest dreams did I expect this. I just felt so confident, so good today. The guys will tell you. I told them before, during the warmup, 'I got it going today.' It was like when you're playing golf and you know every putt's going in. Even the three incompletions, I felt good. I wouldn't even want to take those back."

Playing a key role in Simms' performance was the decision by the Broncos defense to shut down Morris. Taking advantage of that call, our offense went with play-action passes to counter their alignment. Simms threw on nine of our offense's first 11 plays and didn't miss a pass.

On top of that, our offensive line kicked ass that day. Simms was hardly touched by a pretty good Denver defense.

One stat from that day our defense took pride in was the fact Elway finished as the Broncos' leading rusher with 27 yards on six carries. All told they gained just 52 net yards on the day.

Once the game ended, the Rose Bowl turned blue with Giants fans everywhere celebrating the franchise's first title in 30 years.

What a fitting end to a special season.

Yes, 1986 was a good year for the Giants. After the Seattle game in Week 7 when we lost 17–12 at their place, nobody else played with us. We had everything clicking. We were just a better team than everybody we played.

In 2011, Bill Belichick, our defensive coach on the '86 team, took part in a 25th-anniversary celebration for that team and he told ESPN.com, "It was awesome...special group. Unselfish, it was a very competitive group, they loved to practice, they played hard. We had a lot of great players and they fed off each other. Honestly, I think I learned something from every guy. Our defense understood the team concept. The corners knew what the linebackers were doing. The linebackers knew what the nose guard was doing. The nose guard knew it....They had different styles, different things worked for them better than some other guys."

Perhaps his most telling recollection was this: "Our depth was remarkable really, how much talent we had, particularly on the front seven. I learned one thing...they'll make you a good coach."

1991 Divisional Playoff Game

January 13, 1991
Giants 31, Bears 3

A lot of the experts counted us out once we reached the playoffs after the 1990 season.

Some thought we were getting too old. Some thought the other teams were just better. Most thought we couldn't advance in the play-offs because our quarterback and leader, Phil Simms, got injured and was out for the season.

Bill Parcells had no other choice but to throw our backup quarter-back, Jeff Hostetler, into the fire. Along with that move, our offense went to a more conservative approach, which meant the defense had to step it up.

We did.

We opened the playoffs against the Chicago Bears.

We had respect for the Bears. Even though they had lost four of their last six games, they finished the season 11–5 and they beat the Saints 16–6 in a Wild Card game leading up to our game.

Meanwhile, we had won three of our last six to finish at 13–3 before enjoying a bye week. Sometimes a bye week is not the best situation. You can get stale with a week off in a lot of sports. However, in pro football, you get so beat up during the season that a week off heading into the playoffs is an advantage. Everyone on the team has had some kind of injury by the end of the season. That week off allowed us to heal as much as we could in a week.

A record crowd of 77,025 showed up to watch us play in 32 degrees with a wind chill of 15 mph. Bears weather.

We were able to grab an early lead thanks to Mark Collins. Our cornerback intercepted a pass from Mike Tomczak when the ball popped out of his receiver's hands. Once Collins had the ball, he returned it 11 yards to the Bears' 34. That led to a 46-yard Matt Bahr field goal that kissed the left upright before falling through for three points.

The next time we got the ball, Hostetler led us on a 75-yard drive that took nine plays. On the final play of the drive, Hostetler found Stephen Baker for a 21-yard touchdown to put us up 10–0.

You don't want to fall behind a team that had a defense like we did in weather like that. But that's the situation we put the Bears in.

They had an opportunity to score a touchdown in the second quarter when they had the ball on our 1-yard line. On fourth down they decided to go for it, handing the ball to their fullback, Brad Muster. Our tackle, John Washington, sealed the left side of the line and put the first lick on Muster. Carl Banks assisted on the play, and they lost a yard to give us the ball.

Later in the quarter they got a field goal to cut our lead to seven points, but Hostetler found Howard Cross on a 5-yard touchdown pass to put the score at 17–3 heading into the half. We didn't really need to play the second half. The game felt like it was over at the intermission.

Our defense performed well, holding the Bears to 27 yards on 16 carries, completely shutting down their tailback Neal Anderson. He'd gone past 1,000 yards on the season, but he only gained 19 yards on 12 carries against us.

We added another goal-line stand and we stopped them on fourth down four times on the afternoon.

Meanwhile, Hostetler was beginning to grow into the position in his third start of the season. He completed 10 passes in 17 attempts for 112 yards. Our running game helped him along as well. Ottis Anderson led the way with 80 yards on 21 carries.

Ottis' role grew significantly after our rookie tailback Rodney Hampton fractured his left leg.

At the end of the day, we scored 31 points, which equaled our season high. And we put ourselves within one win of returning to the Super Bowl.

1991 NFC Championship

January 20, 1991
Giants 15, 49ers 13

W e faced a major road block in our goal of reaching our second Super Bowl in the 1991 NFC Championship Game: the San Francisco 49ers.

The 49ers had gone to the previous two Super Bowls, and had won both convincingly. On top of that, we entered the game having lost our last four regular-season games against the 49ers. One of those had come weeks earlier when they beat us 7–3 in San Francisco.

We'd lost to them during the 1989 season in an offensive kind of game and the game we'd lost in San Francisco was a defensive contest. So I figured it was about time for us to get the job done against those guys. On top of that, we'd missed the playoffs for two straight years after winning our first Super Bowl, and we'd gotten bounced by the Los Angeles Rams in the first round the year before. We felt like we were due.

Joe Montana still played quarterback for the 49ers in 1991. That guy was a clutch quarterback. When the game was on the line, he was a pretty good guy to have in your huddle. Sometimes the bounces have to go your way and the hunches need to turn out right. That's what happened to us that day.

We even managed to overcome a potential big play going the other way.

In the third quarter, our cornerback, Everson Walls, was covering John Taylor, and he thought he could make the pick. Instead, the play turned into a 61-yard touchdown. You couldn't really fault Everson; he tried to make a play that would have put us up and he just missed. But it put us behind 13–6.

Matt Bahr kicked his third field goal of the game to cut their lead to 13–9 before we started the fourth quarter. That's when things got interesting.

Leonard Marshall knocked Montana out of the game when he hit him from behind with nearly 10 minutes left in the fourth quarter. Montana broke a finger on the play and suffered a bruised chest. We'd hit Montana a lot that day. There wasn't anything dirty about it. Just hard-nosed football.

The way both defenses were playing, you wondered if Montana leaving the game would even matter. We needed a spark and we got it from the guy in charge.

With just over six minutes left the game, Bill Parcells, who was perhaps the most conservative coach in the NFL, decided to roll the dice.

We were facing fourth down and we needed two yards for a first down at our own 46. Parcells sent in the punt team, but instead of Sean Landeta getting the snap, linebacker Gary Reasons, who was the signal-caller on the play, called his own number. The former high school running back got the ball and he took off through a huge hole on the right side of the line. Taylor finally tackled him at the 49ers' 24 after he'd gained 30 yards on the play.

That set up Bahr's fourth field goal of the game to bring us within one point at 13–12. We were suddenly in a better position to take the lead since we didn't need to score a touchdown to do so.

Parcells always gave Reasons the option to call a fake punt. He'd called Reasons over before the play and told him that if he saw an opening, take off. He saw an opening, and that's what he did. Reasons later said the run was his longest since high school.

The 49ers had messed up on the play—they had just ten players on the field at the time. Bill Romanowski was the missing man. He'd gotten injured and nobody had filled in for him. The gap Reasons ran through would likely have been plugged by Romanowski. The 49ers actually tried to call a timeout to send in another player, but they weren't able to do so.

Still, we needed a break if we wanted to win the game. Steve Young, who had taken over for Montana, completed a 25-yard pass to their tight end, Brent Jones, before Roger Craig gained 11 yards on two caries for a first down at our 40. But on the next play, Young gave the ball to Craig and he got hit by Erik Howard, our nose tackle. The ball popped into the air and I grabbed it. We still had a chance.

Jeff Hostetler moved us up the field by throwing 19- and 13-yard completions to Mark Bavaro and Stephen Baker. Several plays later we were calling time out with four seconds left. We were leaving the game up to Bahr. He would determine whether or not we were going to the Super Bowl. When he lined up for the 42-yard kick, teammates were kneeling and holding hands while we prayed for the game winner. The 49ers tried to freeze him. Even the guys on the field-goal unit wouldn't lock eyes with Bahr. Nobody wanted to jinx him.

The Browns had released Bahr during the preseason and he didn't sign with us until Raul Allegre suffered a groin injury early in the season.

Bahr kicked the ball and it sailed through the uprights. You didn't have to watch the kick to know he'd made it since Candlestick Park went quiet. The only sounds in that place were coming from our sideline.

Bahr had made good on his fifth field goal of the game. The 49ers had not allowed us into their end zone for the second time in a month, but we came away with a 15–13 win.

Allegre had been healthy for the last half of the season, but Parcells decided to stick with Bahr, who set a career high with five field goals in that game. He received a game ball from Parcells, who told the media: "You guys have been trying to run him [Bahr] off the team all year. That was the kick of his life and that's why I gave him a game ball."

We'd finally beaten the 49ers and we were headed to Super Bowl XXV in Tampa. That was a sweet win.

Super Bowl XXV

January 27, 1991
Giants 20, Bills 19

The Buffalo Bills were riding high when we met them in Super Bowl XXV.

Jim Kelly led a high-powered offense that had topped the league in scoring with 428 points (26.75 points per game) and defensive end Bruce Smith led a stingy defense en route to being named AP Defensive Player of the Year in 1990. Buffalo allowed just 263 points during the regular season, so that's a differential of 165 points or just over 10 points per game.

Most of their action came from a no-huddle offense, which allowed them to take a quick look at the defense.

At a press conference the week of the game, Bill Parcells came right out and said he didn't think we could "win a shootout game with Buffalo."

"We have shown we can win methodical games," Parcells said. "If they can play their style and prevent us from playing ours, they have a good chance. They look very strong to me."

Bills coach Marv Levy allowed that he didn't "necessarily want a shootout," either.

"I like percentage football," Levy said. "Percentage football is often confused with being conservative, but it's not the same thing. Bill Parcells isn't conservative....This team doesn't give up. We can play tough football no matter what the pace."

The Super Bowl was played in Tampa during a troubling world climate, given the Gulf War. So security was heightened and we had to get to work to figure out how to stop the Bills.

It turned out to be my final Super Bowl. I'd been to one, so I knew what to expect as far as all the hype. I also knew to expect a major challenge given the team we were playing.

Buffalo came into the game having scored 95 points in its first two playoff games. Having a guy like Parcells calling the shots for a game like that proved to be a great advantage.

The Bills had beaten us 17–13 at our place in mid-December. We ran for 157 yards against them that day and running the football was what Parcells planned to do in our Super Bowl matchup. If we were able to do that successfully, the Bills' offense would remain on the sideline. If they didn't have the ball, they couldn't score, right?

Matt Bahr put us up 3–0 with a 28-yard field goal in the first quarter; Buffalo kicker Scott Norwood matched it with a 23-yarder later in the quarter to tie the game. Don Smith scored from one yard out to give the Bills a 10–3 lead, then Bruce Smith tackled Jeff Hostetler in the end zone to make it 12–3 in the second quarter.

Still, we stuck to the game plan. The next time we had the ball we kept pounding it and refused to go to the air. We had to punt, but at the end of the second quarter, we got something going.

Ottis Anderson had an 18-yard run and Dave Meggett went 17 yards on another. Before you knew it, our offense had gone 87 yards with the final 14 yards being covered by a 14-yard touchdown pass from Hostetler to Stephen Backer to cut Buffalo's lead to 2 points. That drive gave us some momentum going into halftime.

We got the kick to start the second half and started at our 25. What followed was a 14-play drive capped by a one-yard touchdown run by Anderson. Not only did that drive give us the lead at 17–12, it kept the

Bills offense off the field for the first nine minutes of the second half.

They finally got something going after we got stopped on fourth down at their 35. There was only a little over a minute left in the third quarter and Kelly hit three quick passes before the quarter ended. Thomas then bolted for a 31-yard touchdown on the first play of the fourth quarter to give them a 19–17 lead.

Our offense got right back after them following the touchdown. You could see their defense was getting tired.

Once again, our guys pounded them, going 74 yards on 14 plays. Our tight end, Mark Bavaro, had two big catches on the drive accounting for 36 yards and we clipped another seven minutes off the clock before the drive stalled and Bahr put us ahead 20–19 with a 21-yard field goal.

We stopped the Bills on their next possession, but we knew Kelly would come at us one last time and that's what he did on their final possession. They gained 11 yards on a pass from Kelly to Thomas to get the ball to our 29 to set up a 47-yard field goal for Norwood that would win the game.

For some reason, I did not have a doubt in my mind that he was going to miss that kick. We had worked too hard that season. Too many things had come together for us to lose on a field goal. He had too much pressure on him or someone was going to block it or deflect it. But there was no way he was going to make that kick.

Fortunately for us, his kick went wide right, not even a yard outside the goalpost, and we won the game. By the time that kick sailed outside the crossbar, I was halfway to Disneyland.

At the end of the day, we ran 73 offensive plays and held the ball for a Super Bowl–record 40 minutes and 33 seconds. Anderson proved to be our horse, chalking up 102 yards to earn MVP honors. Some of those yards came when he ran over guys and others came thanks to the blocking efforts of our offensive line led by Jumbo Elliott, our left tackle.

We did not commit a turnover and our four scoring drives

accounted for 49 plays and more than 26 minutes. The offense kept the ball a long, long time. We knew once we got ahead, our guys were going to run the tar out of the ball. And that's what they did and that's why we won.

I'm fortunate to have played in two Super Bowls, and to be on the winning team in both of them was even better. A lot of players play their whole careers and never get to one.

I'm often asked to compare the two Super Bowls in terms of which one meant more to me. First, I'll say this. When you're talking about Super Bowls, playing in the game is not as exciting as the chase to get there.

When we played the Broncos in my first Super Bowl, we were easily the best team in the NFL. Not just because we won the Super Bowl, but because we dominated every game in the second half of that season. We were on a mission and, like that old comparison, we were men playing against boys. We had a lot of good things happening in that first Super Bowl.

But the second Super Bowl had to be the most gratifying because we had no idea we were going to get there. We just played hard as a team. You looked at San Francisco. They were a better team than we were. The Buffalo Bills were a better team than us on paper. If you went through the team rankings we were probably the fourth-best team in the league on paper. We were able to able to put it together at the right time and that's what it's all about. Everybody came together. You know, in 1990, those other teams might have been better than us at different positions. But nobody played better than us as a team. We had everything going.

We all had one mind; we all had one goal. Parcells always talked about how it's not about being the best team on paper. It's all about the pieces falling together at the right time. That's what happened for us that year.

CHAPTER 3

THE MEN AND MOMENTS

HARRY CARSON

Harry Carson was a team captain when I joined the Giants in 1981.

Everybody respected him. You had to because of the kind of guy he was. He was quiet, a hard hitter, and a team leader. He didn't miss tackles and he was explosive—a true badass if ever there was one.

The Giants drafted him in the fourth round in 1976 out of South Carolina State, where he'd been a force as a down lineman. Think about this: as a senior, he led his defense to six shutouts. That defense only allowed 29 points the entire season. Talk about some pretty tall cotton.

The Giants needed a linebacker the year they drafted Harry. Even though he'd been a down lineman, they thought enough of him that they figured they could turn him into a linebacker. Pretty good call, I'd say.

At first, he played middle linebacker. Later, when they went to a 3–4 defense, he became an inside linebacker. And the rest is history.

I think what Phil McConkey said summed up Harry best:

> *"There were guys that were faster, and there were guys that hit harder, and there were guys that were stronger than him, but nobody had greater heart. People have been trying to find the formula for a great football player for years and they still can't find it. Harry Carson has it, whatever it is."*

Here's the kind of guy Harry was. During another Giants losing season in 1980, he was ready to pack it in and head home to Florence, South Carolina, after a 28–7 loss to the Rams. He felt embarrassed, and even refused to accept his paycheck because he didn't think he deserved it. Imagine that.

Harry also helped me out by quieting the storm with the veteran Giants players when I held out prior to the start of my rookie season.

We had a pretty solid group of linebackers when I got there with Harry, Brad Van Pelt, and Brian Kelley. They called us the "Crunch Bunch." Harry reigned as the unsung hero of that group. But you didn't mess with Harry. He was physical and had instincts. Where I had the freedom to roam and pretty much do whatever I wanted, Harry had to be disciplined.

Here's what Hall of Fame running back Marcus Allen said about Harry Carson in an interview with the *New York Post:*

> *"He was like this immovable object. At the point of attack, you weren't going very far. It's interesting 'cause I never had problems with Lawrence, I always had problems with the other guys. You could always count on Lawrence for being so aggressive that you could make him miss, that [Carson] was so sound, you had such a difficult time."*

Bill Belichick considered Harry the best all-around linebacker that ever played for him. Harry had presence, man.

After we drafted Carl Banks in the first round of the 1984 draft, I remember sitting outside the trainer's room with Harry when Banks walked by.

Harry looked at Carl with this serious look on his face and asked him something about what he was going to do to get on the field. Then he told him how we had a standard to live up to. You had to take him seriously.

Harry wasn't all serious, though.

After Jim Burt came up with the Gatorade shower by dousing Bill Parcells with the Gatorade cooler at the end of games, Harry kept the tradition going even after Burt decided the spontaneity of the act had run its course. Harry surmised that he needed to do so because of how superstitious Parcells was. Anything that we did that worked, Parcells wanted to do again. So the Gatorade showers continued. And I think Parcells started to look forward to it.

Because of Parcells' superstitious nature, he always wanted Harry at his side during the national anthem. He thought Harry brought us good luck.

Harry retired after the 1988 season. On his resume he had nine Pro Bowls and a Super Bowl, had led the Giants in tackles for five seasons, and had served as a captain for ten of his 13 seasons—all spent with the Giants. He became eligible to be elected to the Pro Football Hall of Fame after the 1993 season. Astonishingly, it took him until 2006 to finally get enshrined.

That journey proved to be a painful one for Harry. By the time he finally got elected, he'd made it clear that he didn't care whether he got elected or not. In 2004 he even requested to have his name removed from the ballot. He didn't care for the Hall of Fame selection process because the media voted and not the coaches and players— the guys who really knew what went on between the lines. Harry was way overdue. There are a few people in the Hall of Fame that waited way too long to get there, and there are some people who probably shouldn't be there. But still, that is what it is.

Harry was gracious in his remarks at the Hall of Fame ceremony, but he later commented about being in the Hall of Fame:

> *The Hall of Fame will never validate me. I know my name will be in there, but I take greater pride in the fact that my teammates looked at me as someone they could count on. I still remember, and I will remember this for the rest of my life, the Super Bowl against Denver. We had three*

> *captains—me, Phil Simms, and George Martin. But when it came time for the coin toss before the game, I started to go out and looked around for those guys. Bill Parcells said to me: 'No. You go. Just you.' And that was about the coolest feeling I've ever had in the world—going out to midfield for the Super Bowl, as the lone captain. There were nine Denver Broncos out there, and me. Just me. An awesome responsibility. The greatest respect.*

On the football field Harry had an all-business attitude. You never knew what to say around him, because you didn't know how he was going to take it. It took Harry and me a while to become friends. Now we talk about once a week. We're really close. We talk about everything. It took us a while to get there, but the guy is true blue. I'm honored to call him my friend.

No matter what I got into, any trouble or anything, Harry always supported me because he considered me family. He counted all of his teammates on the Giants as family. And he didn't just talk the talk. He walked the walk. When Doug Kotar was diagnosed with cancer early in the 1980s, Harry was the guy who got all of the players to visit him. When Doug died, Harry was the guy who made sure a scholarship fund was set up for his kids.

Harry showed up at my Hall of Fame induction in 1999 even though we'd had a rift. When I spoke that day, I said, "Harry Carson came out for me today, and that's the classiest thing I've ever seen in my life." I added: "Harry, thank you, thank you. I love you, man. I love you." And that's the way I still feel today.

BRAD VAN PELT

B rad Van Pelt is one of the most incredible athletes I've known. But as good of an athlete as he was, he was an even better person. Everybody loved to be around him. You never saw him when he wasn't smiling. Brad was one of the good guys.

Brad played everything—football, baseball, and basketball—while at Owosso (Michigan) High School. How good of an athlete was he?

"There wasn't a sport he couldn't play and excel at," Brad's high school coach, George Ihler, told the *Saginaw News*.

He could even play fast-pitch softball. Hitting against a really good fast-pitch pitcher is almost impossible. Most guys can't put their bat on the ball the first time they face a fast-pitch pitcher, even if the pitcher is any good.

"Eddie Feigner, the softball pitcher who called himself 'The King,' came to Owosso when Brad was just 18," Ihler said. "Brad took him deep three times. After the game, Eddie offered him a job."

Brad became a two-time All-America defensive back at Michigan State and became the first defensive player to win the Maxwell Award as the nation's top player.

He played baseball and basketball for the Spartans, too.

Basketball was considered the weakest of his three sports. But he played power forward for three seasons for the Spartans and I've heard some say he had NBA potential. As a right-handed pitcher on the baseball team, he helped lead the Spartans to a Big Ten champi-onship in 1971 and was a good enough pitcher to be drafted by the St. Louis Cardinals. A lot of football people thought he might play professional baseball, which hurt him in the NFL Draft. No doubt that's the only reason a player of his status was still available when the Giants drafted him in the second round of the 1973 NFL Draft.

"You're talking an All-Pro football player who started on the Michigan State basketball team and played on the baseball team," Ihler said. "If he hadn't signed to play [pro] football [and missed the spring sports], he would have won nine letters."

When he first got to the Giants, they really didn't know what to do with him. Were they going to leave him in the defensive backfield? Or was he too big for that? Fortunately for Brad and the Giants, Bill Arnsparger, who coached the team from 1974 through 1976, decided to make him a strong-side linebacker. He adapted well to the position change and he thrived.

Brad went on to play 14 seasons in the NFL, becoming a five-time Pro Bowl linebacker. The first 11 of those seasons were with the Giants and he was named the team's Player of the Decade for the 1970s.

You couldn't miss Brad on the football field. You always notice athletes like him, plus he had good size at 6'5", 235 pounds. If that wasn't enough, he wore No. 10, which technically wasn't a number linebackers were allowed to wear according to the NFL rules. But he'd worn the number in college, where he was also the backup kicker. Since he assumed the backup kicker duties with the Giants, too, the league let him wear the number. He always considered the number to be lucky for him.

He'd been in the league eight years by the time I joined the Giants in 1981. I was fortunate that he was on the team when I came aboard, because he helped me a lot. I had a lot to learn my rookie season and he didn't mind helping. Being helpful was part of his nature.

Brad had always been All-Pro and he could definitely play the run and all of that stuff. But when I came, the other teams stopped running at me and started running at him, and he used to get pissed off. He'd say, "Now you're making my job twice as hard."

I respected him, admired him, and most important, considered him a good friend.

Unfortunately, Brad only got to play on one winning team during his time with the Giants. That came when we made the playoffs in 1981. It's too bad; he deserved better.

Once Carl Banks joined the Giants in 1984, Brad got traded to the Vikings for running back Tony Galbreath. He ended up not playing for the Vikings, but he went on to spend two seasons with the Raiders before playing his last season in 1986 for the Browns.

In later years, Brad got involved with some of his old Michigan State teammates to help develop an orphanage in Matamoros, Mexico.

I consider myself lucky to have been a part of another one of his charity ventures when the "Crunch Bunch" reconvened in 2004 to promote a Habitat for Humanity housing project in Puebla, Mexico. We assisted more than 3,000 volunteers who built 150 houses. We even met former president Jimmy Carter on that trip.

I'll never forget the phone call I got from Brian Kelley on February 19, 2009, when he told me Brad had died of a heart attack at his home after playing a round of golf. He was only 57. His fiancée found him and reported that he had a smile on his face. That's Brad.

Giants owner John Mara told the *Daily News* that Brad was one of the greatest players in Giants history, and he added: "If you look at those years, our teams were as bad as could possibly be. We really had some awful teams in the 1970s. He was the one guy who was consistently a good player. It's a shame he left us before our climb back to respectability. I always felt bad he couldn't share in that success."

We only played together for three seasons and he's one of the greatest players I ever played with. He taught me so many lessons on and off the field. In a 2004 interview with Giants.com, Brad said: "I feel as comfortable with [the Crunch Bunch, Harry Carson, Brian Kelley, and me] as I do with my brothers. Obviously, your brothers are your brothers. But these three are probably the closest thing to them. Brian and I played 11 years together. I played nine with Harry. Lawrence being the guy, it didn't take long for him to fit right in and become one of the guys. I can't really explain why, but they're the only three I stay close with."

We did so much together over the years, whether we were attending events, golfing, or whatever. So he's been missed by all of us. If you knew Brad, you loved him, simple as that. I'll always remember him as a unique individual who could always put a smile on my face.

BRIAN KELLEY

On the "Crunch Bunch" we had Harry Carson, who was the team captain; Brad Van Pelt, who was one of the best athletes I've ever seen; and then there was Brian Kelley.

While you wanted approval from Harry, because he was the team leader, you had to have the approval of Brian, because he called the signals.

I got cussed out by the coaches many times and it never fazed me. But the one time I got cussed out by Brian Kelley, that was a whole different thing right there. I had to step up my game after Brian Kelley cussed me out.

You always hear things about Brian being the sleeper of the Crunch Bunch. And I suppose that's true, because Harry and I both got into the Hall of Fame and Brad made five Pro Bowls, but man, that guy was a football player—a smart one, too. He was the guy who put us all in position. Most of the time I'd ask him, "Where do I go on this play?" Brian was the brains behind the group.

When Brian joined the Giants in 1973, he was a long shot to make the team.

You don't see a lot of players who are selected with the 353rd pick get the best shots to make the team, particularly if they played college football at a place like Division II California Lutheran University.

Brian had played defensive end and tight end at Sunny Hills High

School in Fullerton, California. When it came time to go to college, he thought about going to a nearby junior college, but his brother intervened.

Brian always looked up to his older brother, who was like a father to him, and he convinced him to join him at tiny Cal Lutheran in Thousand Oaks, California, not far from their hometown. That turned out to be a great decision for Brian.

With Brian leading the way, Cal Lutheran won the NAIA National Championship in his junior year. By the time he was a senior, he stood 6'3", 225 pounds, and he led them to another championship game, which they lost even though Brian was named the MVP. Despite all of that, and the fact he'd earned All-American honors as a senior, he still wasn't in great demand.

According to the story, the only reason the Giants drafted him was because Giants assistant Jim Garrett, a former Dallas Cowboys assistant, had seen him play. And he might not have ever seen him play had Brian not earned extra cash during college working for the Cowboys. He'd pick up new Cowboys players at the Los Angeles airport along with reporters who covered the team and he'd drive them to the Cowboys' training camp, which was in Thousand Oaks. He also worked security for the team and carted players who had been cut to the airport.

If you've ever been around Brian on a football field, it would be hard to imagine him being a long shot. I mean, the guy could hit. But that's the way he started his career. He managed to earn a roster spot and by 1974 he led the team in tackles, which he did for three straight seasons.

He knew everything that was going on during the game. With him on the field, you felt like you had a defensive coordinator playing beside you. He knew the right scheme to go with everything. It was amazing to have him directing the defense and seeing how he would react when the quarterback called an audible. And he did all of that while also helping out everybody else. It takes quite a leader to be able to do his job and see that everybody else is doing theirs, too.

Unfortunately, Brian didn't get to experience a lot of winning on the Giants. They didn't win many games during his first eight seasons. So I was happy that he was able to get a taste of winning in 1981 when we went 9–7 and earned a spot in the playoffs. He always called that the highlight of his career.

I was fortunate to have been able to play three seasons with Brian. The Giants traded him to the San Diego Chargers after the 1983 seasons for an undisclosed draft choice. Time waits for no one, even the mainstay of a group of linebackers who were generally regarded as the best in the NFL. Brian started every game at inside linebacker in 1983 and he finished second on the team with 114 tackles. Of course we went 3–12–1 in 1983, which prompted change.

Initially, the Giants explained that they made the deal to give more playing time to a second-year linebacker we had named Robbie Jones. Truth be known, Brian wasn't the fastest guy on the field. So despite his superior football intellect, he had begun to get fewer and fewer reps in passing situations.

The Chargers cut Brian in the fall of 1984 and he never played again. So he spent all of his 11 seasons with the Giants. Like everybody in the Crunch Bunch, I've remained close friends with Brian, enough of a good friend to give him the needle when appropriate.

Brian got elected to the College Football Hall of Fame in 2010, which is a really nice honor. When I talked to Brian on the phone to congratulate him, I couldn't resist telling him to call me once he got inducted into the Pro Football Hall of Fame.

GARY REASONS

Gary Reasons is another one of the great linebackers I played with on the Giants.

Gary came to the Giants in the fourth round of the 1984 draft out of Northwestern State, where he'd been a three-time Division I-AA All-America selection. He spent eight years with the Giants before playing his final season in the NFL with the Bengals in 1992.

We didn't miss a beat having him in the lineup. He started a lot of games for us, and he made some big plays that Giants fans still remember. Two in particular come to mind.

In 1989, we were playing a December game against the Broncos in Denver. The game took place in Week 14 and we carried a two-game losing streak into that one. If we wanted to win the NFC East, we knew we had to win because the Eagles were right there with us.

Eight inches of snow had fallen on Mile High Stadium, and the outcome of the game came down to another goal line stand.

We didn't have much of a pregame that day since the tarp covered the field until about an hour before kickoff. The temperature sat in the 20s and the wind-chill factor was below zero. If that wasn't enough, once we started playing, the field got slushy. I didn't play much that day because I was nursing a bad ankle. Gary more than made up for my absence with the play he made.

We were up 14–0 late in the third quarter, but the Broncos had the ball at our 2 on second down. A touchdown would have put them right back in the game. They picked up a yard on the next two downs, leaving them with a fourth-down situation where they needed to pick up about a foot for the score. They had to go for it.

Even though we'd lost to the Eagles the week before, we'd managed a successful goal-line stand in the third quarter. So here we were again.

Their running back, Bobby Humphrey, went right and tried to leap over the guard. Gary had pass-coverage responsibilities on the play, but when they lined up in the I formation for a second consecutive time he anticipated the play, leaping to meet Humphrey for a midair collision. Gary planted his helmet in Humphrey's chest and wrapped his arms around him for a loss of a yard. Bill Parcells would say of the play: "It was a big-time hit. It will probably be in the highlight film."

Parcells was right. The play can still be viewed on YouTube.

That might have been the biggest play of the 1989 season. We went on to beat Denver 14–7 that day, pleasing Parcells to no end. Afterward he noted:

"This is one of the great games since I've been here. We had two very disappointing losses that took a lot of starch out of us, but we came out to this place in this weather and won it."

That victory paved the way for us to win our division with a 12–4 record before we lost in the first round of the playoffs to the Los Angeles Rams.

Ironically, in that Denver game Gary picked up two yards on a fake punt, which served as a preview of the other play he's most remembered for, which took place during our 1991 NFC Championship Game against the 49ers at Candlestick Park.

We were losing to the 49ers 13–9 in the fourth quarter when we had to punt. Gary called the plays on the punt team and had the flexibility to call a fake if he thought it would work. He saw what he wanted on this particular occasion and took off running for a 30-yard gain. That turned out to be huge, because it led to a Matt Bahr field goal and brought us within one at 13–12. We went on to win the game 15–13 on a Bahr field goal on the final play to go to the Super Bowl.

Gary Reasons made a lot of big plays with the Giants, but those are the two I'll remember best—as will most Giants fans.

CARL BANKS

When Brad Van Pelt played linebacker for us, I thought Brad was probably the best run linebacker that I had ever seen. So when we drafted Carl Banks in 1984, I was kind of like, *Why did we draft another linebacker? We've got Brad Van Pelt. He's one of the best run defenders I've ever seen.* Well, guess what. We picked up one who was better at stopping the run than Brad. Carl Banks was that good.

You want to talk about protecting that left side, Carl was the guy. As far as a pass rusher, Carl was average at best. But when it came to playing the run, there wasn't anybody who was better than he was. There was nobody I would rather have had on that opposite side than Carl—especially if Brad Van Pelt is not there—because Carl could shut it down.

The Giants drafted Carl out of Michigan State with the third pick of the 1984 draft. They felt they had drafted the best athlete available and that he would be a dominant player in the league. After getting drafted, Carl told the media how excited he was to be joining the Giants, noting, "This gives me the opportunity to play with one of the greatest linebackers in history—Lawrence Taylor. I want to pattern myself after him."

He came to us bearing the nickname "The Killer," a tag his Michigan State teammates gave him after they found out he worked in a cemetery.

Carl looked like he could be a killer on the field, too. He stood 6'4", 235 pounds, and he was athletic. One of my major concerns with him coming on board was whether speed could replace the knowledge and experience of a guy like Kelley, who was a defensive quarterback on the field. Then Van Pelt got traded and that upset everybody, because he'd been one of the best players in team history and it meant that Banks would be the guy to pick up the slack.

At the outset, Carl's play suggested I'd been right. He struggled. But it didn't take that long for us to realize that Parcells had made the right call. We had No. 56 on one side and Banks, No. 58, on the other.

By the time his 12-year career concluded in 1995, he accrued 39.5 career quarterback sacks, made the Pro Bowl in 1987, was named to the second team of the NFL's 1980's All-Decade Team, was the 1989 NFC Defensive Player of the Year, and helped us win two Super Bowls.

During our win over the Broncos in Super Bowl XXI, Carl had 14 tackles, including 10 solo tackles.

Carl had been one of the most vocal critics of our coach, Ray Handley, and his defensive coordinator, Rod Rust, when we went 6–10 in 1992. That probably contributed to his departure prior to the 1993 season. Other factors were involved, too.

Dan Reeves' arrival as the new coach probably had something to do with Carl leaving the team, too. Reeves had coached the Broncos and knew linebacker Michael Brooks. Once he became a free agent, the writing was on the wall. The Giants obviously didn't want to pay Brooks and Carl, who was an unrestricted free agent, which meant he could sign with the team offering the most money for his services.

Carl eventually signed with the Redskins, bringing his nine-year run with the Giants to a close, though Reeves sounded like he actually wanted to keep him when he said, "I didn't think Carl had played in the last year or so like he did when we played the Giants in the Super Bowl. But I thought he could still play, and we were looking forward to bringing him back."

Carl's numbers were down a bit. He made 60 tackles with four sacks in 1992, which paled to when he had 113 tackles with 6.5 sacks in 1986 or 101 tackles with nine sacks in 1987.

Carl loved his time playing for the Giants, saying, "I had nine great years there. I died for the team and for the players on the team. Those are the things I will miss the most."

But he understood the decision, as he told the *Washington Times*: "It's all about business, and I have to respect what the Giants did."

I don't think Carl ever really got the recognition he deserved because so much of the attention was directed my way. But his performance on the other side really allowed me to have the freedom to rush the passer, which is always more glamorous.

He played two years for the Redskins before finishing his career with the Browns in 1995.

Carl always had a thing for fashion, which prompted him to start a clothing company. He'd begun a men's sports apparel brand during his playing days and ventured into the women's market after he retired. Actually, Carl turned out to be quite a businessman, which dated back to his days digging graves at the Gracelawn Cemetery in Flint, Michigan. During that period he studied the owner of the cemetery. Later he studied other businessmen to try and absorb the methods they had used to find success.

Carl also joined former teammates Joe Morris and Harry Carson as part owners of the Arena Football League's New Jersey Red Dogs, he worked as director of player development for the Jets, and he's done a lot of radio work, too.

I'll remember Carl Banks most for being a good, modest, hard-nosed player along with being a great teammate and a good guy.

LEONARD MARSHALL

Who can forget the hit Leonard Marshall put on Joe Montana in the 1991 NFC Championship Game?

The answer to that one is: nobody.

The man won two Super Bowl rings and had 79.5 sacks in 10 years playing for the Giants, but the Montana hit is what most everybody remembers about Leonard.

Leonard played defensive end and his famous hit came in the fourth quarter when he charged in from the blind side to hammer Montana. Anybody can go to YouTube to watch the hit. Leonard's effort on the play is amazing. Initially, their fullback, Tom Rathman, took him down. Leonard crawled on his knees momentarily then crab walked a step or two before getting to his feet and lowering the boom on Montana to force a fumble. Leonard hit him so hard that he bruised the sternum of the future Hall of Fame quarterback. Montana suffered a broken hand, a bruised stomach, and broken ribs on the play, too.

That turned out to be Montana's final play for the 49ers. He moved on to Kansas City the next year and Steve Young became the 49ers' quarterback. Not to be forgotten, we beat the 49ers 15–13 in that game to advance to the Super Bowl. Leonard's play turned out to be one of the biggest of the season.

Leonard would later talk to the *New York Daily News* about the play and said: "It was one of the situations where I was not trying to make a play to injure or hurt him; I was trying to make a football play to help my team win, and it just happened. It was his calling and my destiny to make a football play. It definitely had an impact on his situation in a negative way and you hate to see things happen to a guy like that."

Fox Sports Net ranked the hit as the third-most-devastating hit in NFL history and *The Best Damn Sports Show Period* ranked Leonard's hit as the third-most-devastating hit in all of sports history.

Leonard played 12 seasons in the NFL. All but two were with the Giants, the team he began his career with after getting drafted out of LSU in the second round of the 1983 NFL Draft. After the Giants selected him, Raiders owner Al Davis said the Giants had made the steal of the draft. Leonard would prove the NFL icon correct.

Leonard grew up in Franklin, Louisiana, in a family with seven children. His father, Leonard Sr., never wanted his oldest child, Leonard, to play football. The elder Marshall worked as a foreman at a shipyard and felt like playing football was a waste of time and would prevent his son from doing more productive things. Leonard Sr. later changed his tune after his son played well enough in high school to earn a football scholarship to LSU, where he became an All-America selection to pave the way for a professional career.

"I didn't want to be hanging around on corners," Leonard told the *New York Times*. "'I wanted to do something with the rest of my life, and I thought football was a way. My dad realizes now that I did the right thing. He's proud now."

Leonard reported heavy to his first training camp at around 295 pounds, and he had a penchant for sneaking out to a McDonald's near our training camp at Pace University in Pleasantville, New York. The coaches put him on a diet and one of the coaches began to keep an eye on him so he couldn't get to the Golden Arches. That got him down to around 275 pounds.

He arrived to the NFL better against the run than at rushing the passer, which could be seen in the numbers. He only had half a sack in 1983, his rookie season. His tendency would be to stand tall after the snap rather than trying to stay low so he could gain leverage on the man blocking him.

A lot of college linemen arrived to the NFL without the proper technique, because colleges ran the ball most of the time back then. That's why it's unusual for a rookie defensive lineman to be a really good pass rusher. Strength had been enough for Leonard to succeed at the college level. He'd gotten the job done by throwing a forearm. Our coaches taught him to use his hands first.

Leonard was a hard-nosed player. Nobody worked harder than Leonard Marshall. He would hit the gaps and he knew what he was supposed to do. You knew what you were going to get from him. With a lot of players, you don't know what you're going to get. He knew if he had to hit gap A, he hit gap A. If he had to hit gap B, he hit gap B. Leonard was a smart guy, too, and quickly learned some of the necessary techniques for rushing the quarterback.

In 1984, he finished with 6.5 sacks. And his play against the run continued to be solid. That proved fortunate for us in our 16–13 Wild Card game win against the Los Angeles Rams.

The Rams had running back Eric Dickerson, who had gained 2,105 yards that season, so we knew we had our work cut out stopping him. You could count Leonard among those rising to the occasion.

In the second quarter the Rams had second-and-3 at our 27. Dickerson went left and Leonard got him for a 5-yard loss. They didn't get their first down on third down and had to settle for a field goal.

Later, with approximately 7 minutes left in the game, we had a six-point lead as the Rams faced a second-and-goal at our 4-yard line. The Rams brought in Dwayne Crutchfield and we knew from their tendencies they liked to give him the ball when they brought him into the game. Crutchfield brought a load. He weighed in at around 250 pounds. He could push the pile. Bill Belichick, our linebackers coach at the time, called for us to run our goal-line defense. Leonard hit the guard-tackle gap to dodge the tackle and grabbed Crutchfield right after he got the ball for a 3-yard loss. They completed a short pass on third down, but they had to settle for a field goal, so we dodged the bullet and came away with a 16–13 lead that we were able to maintain for the win.

Leonard continued to improve.

In 1985 he had 15.5 sacks and earned NFL Defensive Lineman of the Year honors. He won the award again the following season when he had 12 sacks. Leonard earned Pro Bowl selections for his performances in the 1985 and 1986 seasons.

In Super Bowl XXI he twice sacked Denver quarterback John Elway in our 39–20 win. And he recorded a sack in our Super Bowl XXV win over the Bills.

The 1992 season turned out to be Leonard's last with the Giants. A part of that had to do with the climate in our locker room under Parcells' successor, Ray Handley. A lot of the players on our defense were not happy with our head coach and expressed their displeasure. Leonard was one of them, so he wasn't a part of the 1993 plans when Dan Reeves took over as our coach. That prompted him to make his exit as a free agent.

After spending his entire career at defensive end, he moved inside to play tackle for the Jets in 1993. He finished his career in 1994 playing tackle for the Redskins.

All told, Leonard had 83.5 career quarterback sacks in the regular season and another twelve sacks in the postseason. That's an average of nearly 10 sacks a season from 1985 to 1991, which is pretty impressive and a big reason why we had such a dominant defense.

Leonard did return to the Giants to sign a one-day contract so he could retire as a Giant. On the day he announced his decision, he noted: "I wanted to retire a Giant because it's where my career began.

They were people who believed in my talents and helped mold me into the man I am today, and I wanted to thank them for that."

Leonard has done all sorts of things since retiring from football. Among them, he wrote a book with CBSsports.com writer William Bendetson: *When the Cheering Stops: Bill Parcells, the 1990 New York Giants, and the Price of Greatness.*

GEORGE MARTIN

George Martin was a great football player and he is a great human being. He cares about people and his actions have always spoken louder than his words.

The Giants got a good one when they selected George out of the University of Oregon in the 1975 NFL Draft. He went on to play 14 years, all with the Giants, and missed only six games in all that time. A pretty remarkable feat considering he played defensive end and the length of time he played in the league.

During that time he had 46 sacks, but remember—sacks were not officially recognized by the NFL until 1982. The Giants credit him with making 96 career sacks. Simply stated, he was one of the best pass rushers in the league. George could sack a quarterback, but he also knew what to do with the ball when it fell into his hands.

He scored seven career touchdowns—two came via fumbles, one came from a lateral return after a blocked field goal, three were returned interceptions, and one came when he caught a touchdown pass in 1980 when he lined up at tight end. Those six defensive touchdowns were good for the most scored by a defensive lineman until Miami's Jason Taylor broke the record in 2006 with his seventh defensive touchdown.

Touchdowns and sacks can be memorable, and George had a pretty nice highlight reel where both were concerned.

George established himself as the NFL's all-time leader in touchdowns for a defensive lineman when he picked one off against the Cardinals in November 1988 and returned it 56 yards for a touchdown to give him five career touchdowns. He added his sixth, and final, defensive touchdown the following season.

We were 9–2 when the Broncos visited us at the Meadowlands on November 23, 1986. If we were going to win the NFC East, we knew we had to keep winning and that meant beating teams like the Broncos. They were a quality team and held a 6–3 lead late in the second quarter. They looked headed for more after Louis Wright recovered a fumble to give them the ball at our 41.

John Elway was giving us fits that day. He finished with 29 completions in 47 attempts for 336 yards. He even ran for 51 yards, including a sneak on that drive that gave the Broncos a first down at our 13. That's when the momentum of the game changed, thanks to George.

Gerald Willhite appeared to be open close to the left sideline, so Elway attempted to get him the ball. George anticipated the action and grabbed the ball out of the air with his left hand before turning up the field. I had a perfect view of the action since I trailed him on the play.

George didn't have the ball tucked away. He held it in his hand like a mason holding a brick. When Elway zeroed in on him at about the 40, I thought he might flip the ball to me. Instead, George stiff armed him and kept going.

Sammy Winder entered the picture around the Broncos' 20, but Mark Collins delivered a key block on the Denver running back. George hurdled over Winder before stumbling into the end zone to complete the 78-yard touchdown run. That's when I jumped on his back and tackled him. Somebody told me that George's return took 17 seconds. George later teased: "When I caught it, it was a bright sunny day. When I got to the end zone, it was cloudy. The weather had changed considerably."

George explained the play to reporters afterward.

"Elway was throwing a lot of swing passes, and he threw one to me," he said. "I saw the ball coming and just stuck up my hand. Then, after I caught it, I wanted to stay near the sideline in case I lost it because it would go out of bounds. I gave Elway a good stiff arm to get away from him and then I thought I might make it all the way."

Parcells called the play "one of the greatest he ever saw," adding, "People forget that Denver had gone the length of the field. The defense was exhausted, and for a lineman who had been chasing Elway for seven or eight plays in a row to run the ball all the way back like that was something else."

That proved to be our only touchdown of the day in a 19–16 win.

George's second really memorable play came in Super Bowl XXI against the same Broncos. Late in the second quarter we were losing 10–7 when George came through. Again, he did so at the expense of Elway.

Elway dropped back to pass from the Broncos' 13, taking him into the end zone. George beat their tackle Ken Lanier on the play and tackled Elway for a safety, giving George his first career safety and cutting the Broncos' lead to 10–9. George suckered Lanier into thinking that he would be going inside on the play.

"He took the bait and I went outside," George told reporters. "It was a great thrill, and I'm sure it gave us a shot in the arm."

We went on to roll the Broncos in the second half to win our first Super Bowl by a score of 39–20.

Everybody loved George. He and his family would always have teammates over for Thanksgiving dinner every year. And he's continued to be that kind of guy since his playing days ended. For example, in 2008, he wanted to raise money for 9/11 victims. So he walked from the George Washington Bridge to San Diego—3,020 miles—to raise approximately $2 million. And when Bill Parcells was inducted into the Hall of Fame, George was the guy he asked to present him at the induction ceremony.

George told ESPN Radio's *The Michael Kay Show* that presenting

Bill was "one of the greatest honors that I'd ever received."

He continued by saying, "It is just something that I never thought would ever happen for me, particularly when you look at the swath of distinguished individuals that he could have selected to induct him into the Hall. So it's a tremendous honor."

That's just the way George Martin thought about himself. We all regarded him as a giant among the Giants.

PEPPER JOHNSON

Pepper Johnson represented the new school—which is now the old school—but it was the new school when he first came to the Giants. New-school guys could go out and have a good time and come back and kick your ass on Sunday. New-school guys came in with the rap music and the big headphones. I used to look at Pepper and tell him, "Turn that shit off!"

Pepper came in and took over for Brian Kelley. That wasn't an easy task and he did well. He played hard-nosed football.

His aunt gave him his nickname after she noticed him putting pepper on his cereal in the morning. Maybe there's something to the pepper diet, because he grew up strong, big, and fast.

After attending high school in Detroit, he played at Ohio State, earning All-America honors his senior year and his teammates named him the defensive MVP in his junior and senior years.

We got him in the second round of the 1986 NFL Draft and he became a big part of the defense that helped us win two Super Bowls.

Pepper played a lot of good football for the Giants. One game that stands out to me is our 1990 win over the Vikings to clinch the NFC East.

A lot of people remember that game because Bill Parcells had kidney stones. Everybody knew he was hurting.

The Vikings brought a five-game winning streak into the game.

And with Rich Gannon at quarterback and Hershel Walker at running back, the Vikings took a 12–10 lead into halftime.

We needed some kind of a spark at that time and Pepper gave us that needed jolt on their first possession of the second half.

The Vikings took the ball up the field putting them at our 7. On second down, Gannon hit Steve Jordan for five yards, but Pepper hammered him to force a fumble that Myron Guyton recovered for us.

After that, the Vikings had the ball seven times and gained only 36 yards in 19 plays with just one first down. We outscored them 13–3 in the second half to take a 23–15 win. He had nine tackles and two assists in that game, too. We had a lot of heroes in 1990 to lead us to an unlikely Super Bowl win. The fumble Pepper forced had to be one of the biggest plays of our season, though.

I also remember a game in Tampa against the Bucs. Pepper had a particularly dominant performance that day.

At that point in the season he only had one sack and we were in Week 13 at the end of November. That didn't stop his greatness from coming through that day, though.

Jeff Hostetler got hurt on a hit to the back by Bucs linebacker Broderick Thomas, so Phil Simms finished the game at quarterback. And I got knocked out of that game early in the second quarter when their running back Gary Anderson chopped down on my knee. Turned out that didn't matter. Pepper took control of the game while Bobby Abrams and Corey Miller took over for me.

When I left the game, Pepper had already recorded a sack. He finished with a team-record 4.5 sacks, made nine tackles, had an interception, and forced a fumble. We won the game 21–14.

The 1992 season turned out to be Pepper's last with the Giants. Like a lot of guys on the defense, he didn't care for the way our coach, Ray Handley, ran the team, and in particular he didn't care for defensive coordinator Rod Rust's system. Pepper became one of the more vocal critics of the situation and once Ray got fired, Pepper said: "You knew it was going to happen. Some guys are meant to be head coaches. I don't know if Ray was.... We had a style we were used to winning with, and Ray wanted to change it. Some spoke about it publicly and others privately. It was a touchy situation."

Whether right or wrong, I think Pepper got labeled as a player they needed to get rid of once Dan Reeves took over. He ended up playing the 1993, 1994, and 1995 seasons for the Browns, who were coached by Bill Belichick at the time. He moved on to the Lions in 1996 before playing the final two seasons of his 13-year career with the Jets. He finished his career with 1,200 tackles, 25.5 sacks, 14 interceptions, 12 forced fumbles, and two Pro Bowl appearances.

After he retired he became a coach. His first stop was as an assistant linebackers coach for the Patriots during the 2000 season, and he's been coaching ever since.

Pepper's son, Dionte, followed his father's footsteps by playing for Ohio State, but he played on the other side of the ball, at fullback. Dionte also was elected as a captain by his Ohio State teammates, making Pepper and him the third father–son captains in Ohio State history.

Dionte went on to play in the NFL for the Arizona Cardinals.

Pepper Johnson is still the same way he always was, hard-nosed and nails. I talk to him all the time to this day. I consider him a good friend.

JIM BURT

Jim Burt is arrogant. Jim's an asshole. Jim's a ballbuster—whatever you want to call him. But if I'm in a game, he's on my team. You understand what I'm saying? He's on my team. He can get on your nerves and he'll fight at the drop of a hat, but on Sunday there's no way I'm going into battle without Jim Burt. You had to respect Jim Burt.

Jim joined the Giants in 1981, the same year as me. Despite being a standout at the University of Miami, he arrived to the team with considerably less hoopla than me. He wasn't even drafted. He signed as a free agent. So the odds of him making the team weren't good. Free agents have more of a chance of making a team these days because there are fewer rounds of the NFL Draft. But back in 1981, there were 12 rounds, which meant there were 332 players selected. Today there are just seven rounds. In the 2015 NFL Draft, 256 players were selected. Get the idea?

Still, Jim managed to hang and impress Bill Parcells, who was the defensive coordinator at the time. He did so by working his ass off in camp. Nobody worked harder. He showed smarts on the field and he was just tough. He knew how to draw attention. If you saw a fight break out during that camp, chances were Jim could be found in the middle of it.

Parcells could motivate. And he knew everything he had to do to get Jim going. For example, on the Thursday before a game, Parcells would have Jim raise a dumbbell off the ground over and over in the weight room to simulate him firing out of his stance and raising his arm at the snap. This would go on for almost an hour. Antics like that worked on Jim. By the time we played a game on Sunday, Jim would be plenty pissed thanks to Parcells, and the guy in front of him paid the price.

Once Parcells became our head coach, Jim definitely became one of his guys.

One of the biggest games we played in my career was our 1986 NFC Divisional Game against the 49ers. In that game, Jim knocked out their quarterback, Joe Montana, on a hit. On the back end of that play, I intercepted Montana's pass and returned the pick for a touchdown. We ended up winning that game 49–3 en route to our first Super Bowl.

In the closing moments of that Super Bowl, when we beat the Broncos 39–20, Parcells told our defense to relax and take our pads off because we had the game in hand. Shortly after that, Jim's five-year-old son was on the field slapping palms with me, leading up to one of the nice moments people remember from Super Bowls past.

Jim kissed Jimmy and put him up on his shoulders and the TV cameras captured every second there on the field at the Rose Bowl. Seeing a "macho guy" like Jim showing affection to his son gave everyone a warm and fuzzy feeling. He got all kinds of letters after that commending him for the public display of affection from a father toward his son.

Jim also invented the Gatorade shower. Obviously, the Gatorade shower has since taken on a life of its own.

After we beat the Redskins on October 20, 1985, Jim dumped a cooler of Gatorade on Parcells. We were 3–3 going into that game and Parcells had been riding Jim's ass all week, telling him that Redskins offensive lineman Jeff Bostic was going to tear his ass up. That pissed off Jim. So when we beat them 17–3, Jim went for the cooler and poured Gatorade on Parcells.

We couldn't believe anybody would do that to Parcells. Jim would say of his ploy: "I was the only one who had the guts to do it without knowing what his reaction was going to be."

Gatorade showers have since become a ritual, as familiar to the end of big games as the victory formation. If you see a Gatorade shower on your sideline, you know you've won the game.

Jim could have a sense of humor, too. In a 24–13 loss to the Eagles in 1988, he got nabbed having a little too much Vaseline on his arms after the Eagles' center, Dave Rimington, told the officials what was going on. Yes, the slippery stuff could help you slip past blockers. Rimington told the ref that the Vaseline was "glazing in the light."

Jim didn't get thrown out of the game or anything; he just had to go to the sideline and wipe himself off. Later, when asked about the episode, he couldn't keep a straight face when he offered an excuse to reporters along the lines of it being cold and that the Vaseline worked as an insulator that helped him retain body heat.

To Rimington's credit, he confessed that he had grown familiar with the Vaseline technique from employing it while at Nebraska.

After the 1988 season, Jim's constant back problems finally prompted Parcells to announce Jim's retirement for him, which was an unusual move. However, Jim opted to continue playing, which he did for the 49ers beginning in 1989. That allowed him to be a part of his second Super Bowl–winning team as the 49ers went to Super Bowl XXIV in 1989 and demolished the Broncos 55–10.

When we went to the Super Bowl in 1991, we defeated the 49ers along the way. That led to some verbal sparring with Jim, who was still as feisty as ever.

Jim had retired for a second time prior to the 1990 season due to a shoulder problem. San Francisco coach George Seifert talked him into playing another season, though. The 49ers had won two consecutive Super Bowls and were shooting to head to the Super Bowl for a third straight year, but we beat them 15–13 in the NFC Championship

Game. During that game, we thought Jim tried to hurt our quarterback Jeff Hostetler.

He defended himself by saying he got caught in between our center and right guard when he rushed on the play and got pushed on his back, which caused him to hit Hostetler. He went so far as to tell the media we could watch the film and if we still had an issue with him we could visit him one by one at his home in New Jersey. Knowing Jim, you knew he meant what he said.

He retired after that game, finishing his career with 20 quarterback sacks and a Pro Bowl appearance in 1986.

Later, when Parcells was the head coach of the Dallas Cowboys—yes, those Cowboys, the ones hated by every Giants fan—he decided to install the 3–4 defense. He called to ask Jim and Carl Banks to join the Cowboys at training camp to help teach the defense, and they did.

Jim Burt was one of those guys that every team has. You looked at him and figured, *This guy has no business being on the football field.* He was only 6'1", 260 pounds or so. But he's out there and one day you realize you can't do anything without him.

OTTIS "O.J." ANDERSON

Ottis Anderson became a big star at the University of Miami. A bruising running back, he had some flash, too.

While playing for the Hurricanes, he broke Chuck Foreman's career rushing record and became the first player in the school's history to surpass 1,000 yards rushing in a season. He did that his senior year in 1978 when he put 1,266 yards on the board en route to All-American honors.

He was a year or two ahead of me when I played at North Carolina, and we all knew who he was.

Ottis didn't miss a beat when he got to the NFL in 1979, and he still had a lot of good football left in the tank by the time the Giants acquired him from the St. Louis Cardinals early in the 1986 season.

I once heard Ottis describe himself as an unpredictable runner and say that he would run off other players' reactions. It was hard to figure out what he was going to do, since he said he didn't even know what he was going to do once he had the football.

The Cardinals picked him with the eighth overall pick of the first round in the 1979 NFL Draft. You could say he let everybody know he'd arrived in his first game in the NFL. Ottis ran for 193 yards on 21 carries against the Dallas Cowboys, including a 76-yard jaunt for a touchdown.

He finished his rookie season with 1,605 rushing yards, earning a

Pro Bowl selection, first-team All-Pro honors, and the NFL Offensive Rookie of the Year award.

In addition to his total rushing yards his rookie season, which broke Earl Campbell's mark of 1,450 set in 1978, he set three additional rookie records by running for 100 yards nine times, becoming the first rookie to average over 100 yards rushing per game, and tallying 331 carries, which established a rookie mark and left him just eight carries shy of the NFL record for any player.

Ottis packed a load at 6'2", 225 pounds, and he sustained his brilliance. Following his rookie season, he ran for 1,352 yards. All told, he rushed for over 1,000 yards in five of his first six seasons. The strike-shortened 1982 season proved to be the only season he did not reach 1,000 yards in that span, and he would have likely done so since he logged almost 600 yards in the eight games he did play that season.

Talk about a workhorse. In 1984, he caught 70 passes. That meant he handled the ball on 359 plays that season. Man, that's a lot of football. So it wasn't surprising that injuries eventually entered the picture.

Despite having a lot of talent on those Cardinals teams, they never went anywhere. Ottis caught 70 passes primarily because their quarterback, Neil Lomax, used him as a safety valve to avoid taking a loss. Still, that left Ottis exposed to get pounded a lot by opposing defenses. And any time you get injured in the NFL, you're leaving yourself wide open to have somebody else take your job. That's kind of what happened with Ottis in St. Louis.

The Cardinals had a backup by the name of Stump Mitchell.

In 1981, they drafted him out of Citadel in the ninth round. He didn't get to play that much until Ottis went down with an injury at the end of the 1985 season. That allowed Mitchell to start eight games, and he showed well, running for 1,006 rushing yards and seven touchdowns.

Prior to the 1986 season, Mitchell got an offer from the Arizona Outlaws to jump to the USFL. With Ottis looking a little worn and

Mitchell coming off his 1985 season, the Cardinals opted to sign Mitchell to a three-year, $1.2 million contract. Eventually they decided to re-sign Ottis to a new contract, as well. Supposedly there were a lot of incentives in the deal that put him in the range of $600,000 a year.

Anderson went into the 1986 season as the Cardinals' all-time leading rusher and the 11th leading rusher in NFL history. But anybody who did the math could have figured that this one wasn't going to end well. The Cardinals weren't going to have a backfield with both Mitchell and Ottis. Both were better running the ball than blocking and the Cardinals had two really good blocking backs in Ron Wolfley and Earl Ferrell. So you just knew either Ottis or Mitchell would likely be gone if they got through training camp with both healthy.

Meanwhile, Joe Morris was holding out for us, which got the Giants interested in talking to the Cardinals about acquiring Ottis. The Giants had wanted him all the way back to when they decided to select Phil Simms in the 1979 Draft instead of him. But that had been a tough call and both players ended up having great careers.

Eventually the Giants and Morris got on the same page and he had another quality season for us. Predictably, the situation in St. Louis got dicey early.

Ottis demanded to get traded after the Cardinals opened the 1986 season with a 16–10 loss to the Los Angeles Rams. He expressed his displeasure at getting lifted from the game, and that's when he told the Cardinals about wanting to be traded.

In early October, we got Ottis from the Cardinals for two undisclosed 1987 draft choices.

I can tell you one thing. The sentiment on our team was we'd rather be playing alongside Ottis than against him.

Ottis got caught up in a numbers game with us initially. Morris was our main back, so Ottis didn't get a lot of carries. He did manage to run for a touchdown in our Super Bowl XXI win over the Broncos that season.

In 1989, Ottis won the NFL Comeback Player of the Year award when he ran 325 times for 1,023 yards and scored a career-high 14 rushing touchdowns. He remained our top running back in 1990 when we continued to go with a ball-control approach on offense and used that to win Super Bowl XXV. In that game, our offense had the ball for more than 40 minutes. Ottis ran for 102 yards and a touchdown while winning MVP honors.

Ottis shouldered a big load with us. That whole offense did what it had to do to win. You needed a bruising back in those days; that's what the NFC East was all about. Seemed like every team had a bruiser running back, such as Washington, which had John Riggins, and some of the guys they had in Philadelphia. We always had bruisers for running backs. Nowadays, it's not that way. In order to win when I played, you had to have an offense that could run the football, especially in December and January.

Ultimately, Rodney Hampton put Ottis out to pasture in 1991. He retired after the 1992 season. Consider this: he fumbled just three times in 739 touches while a Giant.

That's crazy.

MARK BAVARO

Mark Bavaro. I'm telling you, the guy was a warrior. He was the kind of guy you wanted to go to battle with, anytime, anywhere.

Initially, I underestimated him.

"Rambo" came to the Giants in 1985. Back then, you'd hit guys in practice. None of this shoulder-pads-and-shorts shit. I mean, there was some popping going on.

Mark and I used to go at it every day. He was physical, but I didn't consider him much more than that. I didn't think he was a good receiver. I thought he was just a blocker.

Boy, was I wrong.

He just got better and better. He became a better blocker and more physical—the guy did everything he was supposed to do and more in the weight room. And he turned into a great receiver.

Rambo never showed any expression. He looked like Sylvester Stallone, so he got the nickname he hated, Rambo, and it stuck. But he had a lot going on in his head, too. The dude was smart. He even wrote a book once he retired.

Mark had been an All-America selection at Notre Dame before the Giants picked him up in the fourth round of the 1985 NFL Draft. He didn't start right away, but it didn't take long. If I'd known anything about him before he became a Giant, his success wouldn't have surprised me.

Not only did he become a high school All-American at Danvers High School in Danvers, Massachusetts, he also stood out in track and field.

At Notre Dame, he began to establish himself as a physical guy who could play through pain. In Gerry Faust's *Tales from the Notre Dame Sideline*, the former Notre Dame head coach said of Mark, "He plays with pain better than any player I've seen in my 37 years of coaching."

Zeke Mowatt started at tight end for us in Mark's rookie season. But he got injured before the start of the season and Mark stepped right in.

Bill Parcells loved the guy. Why wouldn't he? He played physical football, did as he was told, and kept his mouth shut.

At the end of the year, his numbers validated that Mark could play and Parcells knew talent. Mark caught 37 passes and four touchdowns.

Mark was a religious dude. Whenever he scored a touchdown he'd go down to one knee in the end zone and motion the sign of the cross. In a game against the Bengals, Phil Simms threw for 513 yards. Mark set a team record that day with 12 catches.

Mark remained the starting tight end in 1986 even though Mowatt returned.

Simms loved throwing to the guy. And there wasn't any of that sophomore-jinx shit with Bavaro. He earned his first Pro Bowl appearance in 1986 when we won the Super Bowl. The 66 passes he caught that season set a new Giants record for tight ends. I'm telling you, he did it all with a hell-bent style that spelled toughness. Everybody fed off the way he played. There were times when it seemed like the whole defense was on his back trying to bring him down. He broke his jaw that season and continued to play even though he had to drink his food through a straw.

The one play of Mark's that always stands out came during that 1986 season. We were losing a Monday-night game 17–0 to the 49ers at San Francisco when we went to the locker room at the end of the first half. We were 10–2 at that point in the season.

Parcells was pissed at halftime and cut loose on the offense. He told them how San Francisco's intensity level was much higher than ours. Our offensive coordinator, Ron Erhardt, took some heat, too. Parcells told him in no uncertain terms that the offense needed to score some points.

Mark turned out to be the guy who turned around the intensity level after he caught a short pass over the middle.

Ronnie Lott was no stranger to contact, but the future Hall of Fame safety couldn't bring Mark down. Nobody could. More 49ers kept climbing on his back, but he just kept chugging along. The play ended up going for 31 yards.

We didn't allow the 49ers to score in the second half and the offense came in with three touchdowns to lead us to a 21–17 win. Mark caught seven passes for 98 yards that night. None was bigger than that catch across the middle. That might have been one of the biggest plays of the year.

Mark didn't miss a game in his first four seasons in the league. You just knew that couldn't last given the way he played, though. Particularly considering how many people he ran over. If you're on defense, you take your pound of flesh against a guy like that when he's catching the ball and he's vulnerable. Pretty soon that caught up to him.

He didn't play in half our games in 1989, but he returned strong in 1990, which helped us win our second Super Bowl. Everybody remembers a couple of big catches he made during that game to give us first downs and help us defeat the Bills 20–19.

The drive that led to Matt Bahr's game-winning 21-yard field goal saw our offense march 74 yards in 14 plays. Mark caught passes of 17 and 19 yards from Jeff Hostetler during that critical drive to finish with five catches for 50 yards.

After dealing with a knee problem for the entire 1990 season, he was cut by the Giants prior to the 1991 season. He ended up playing three more seasons with the Eagles and Browns before retiring in 1995.

Like I said, Mark is a smart guy. So once he got out of football he became a businessman, starting out as a sales trader for an equity block-trading firm. Away from work he's like me—he loves to play golf. Competing on the golf course isn't competing on the football field, but it allows you to compete in something.

He also wrote that novel I mentioned. It came out in 2008 and is titled *Rough & Tumble*. He'd actually started writing while he was still playing.

In the book, Dominic Fucillo is the main character. He plays tight end for the Giants, is religious, and had a boatload of injuries. Sound familiar?

Looking back, Mark had his stuff together. He remained humble even when he became a star and he kept his blue-collar work ethic. This guy had the heart of a lion. If you ever went to battle and this guy wasn't on your team, then you were at a disadvantage. I'm telling you what. He was all man, because he was a player.

Michael Strahan

Michael's first year in the league was my last. By that time, I was feeling the wear and tear on my body and I wasn't into football as much.

Michael's father was a major in the U.S. Army, so he attended high school in Germany, where his father was stationed. Then his father sent him to Houston to live with his uncle Arthur Strahan, who had played in the NFL. Michael must have showed 'em something because after one season of high school football he earned a scholarship to Texas Southern.

The Giants picked him in the second round of the 1993 draft, and he didn't know what the hell he was doing when he first got to the Giants. But I watched him grow. He had a mean streak in him and that toughness you need. With that smile he's got—and that little gap between his front teeth—you wouldn't think he'd be a mean guy or a physical guy. But he was. And he came in and worked hard.

Michael had a foot injury his rookie season and only played in nine games. The following year he became the starting right defensive end and he recorded 4.5 sacks—and a team-high 7.5 the following year. He was off and running for a great career.

I always liked the way Michael showed respect to people. I mean, he respected the hell out of me when he first started. And he didn't have to do that. When we hung out, I tried to offer him some advice

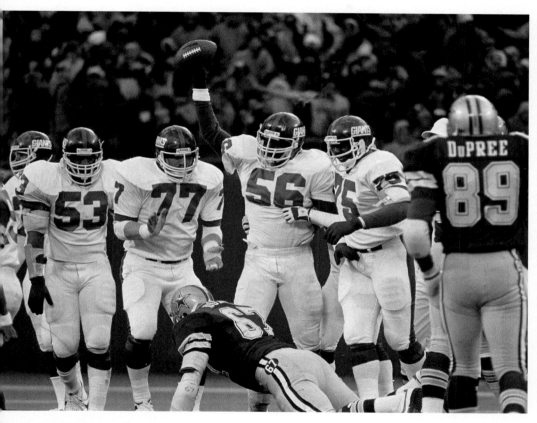

Lawrence Taylor made an impact on the Giants defense right away in 1981. He recovered a fumble in a game against the Dallas Cowboys, and the team earned a playoff berth.

Lawrence Taylor, pictured here in 1988, was a ferocious pass rusher, as evidenced by the blood on his pants.

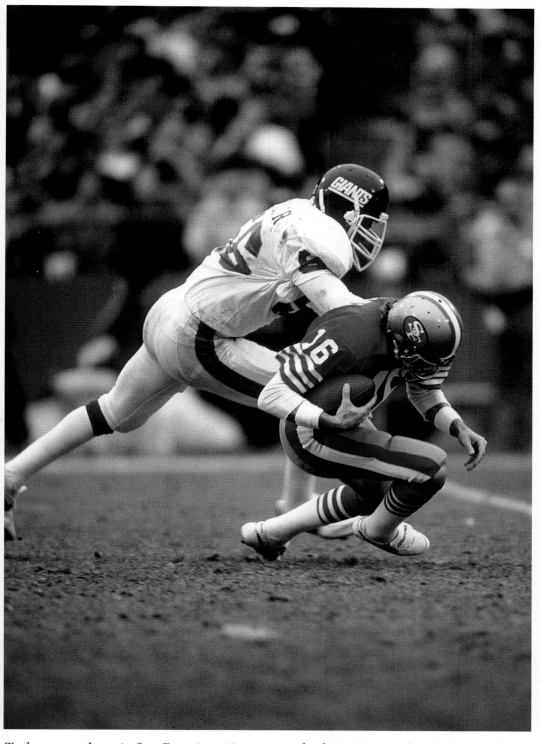

Taylor was a thorn in San Francisco 49ers quarterback Joe Montana's side during their shared time in the league. Here, Taylor sacks Montana in the 1984 NFC Divisional Game between the Giants and 49ers.

Taylor, pictured here with two other members of the "Big Blue Wrecking Crew," Mark Collins (25) and Carl Banks (58).

Taylor talks to the media at Super Bowl XXI in January 1987.

New York Giants quarterback Phil Simms (11) embraces Taylor after the Giants defeated the Denver Broncos 39–20 to win Super Bowl XXI.

In 1987, Taylor became the first defensive player to win the Schick Trophy for the NFL's Most Valuable Player.

Taylor was inducted into the NFL Pro Football Hall of Fame on August 7, 1999, in his first year of eligibility.

about different things, and luckily, he didn't listen to any of it. No, I'm just kidding.

Michael turned out to be a great athlete. I mean, he's in the Hall of Fame. But he's also a great person. That doesn't mean I'm ever going to let up telling him that his sacks record for the Giants is tainted. Or, at the very least, there should be an asterisk next to his name.

I mean, yes, Michael holds the team's sacks record, but my career total of 132.5 isn't accurate since sacks were first recorded after the 1981 season, a year after my rookie season. I had 9.5 sacks that season. That means I had 142 career sacks, which is a half a sack more than Michael's 141.5. And don't you think I don't remind him.

I liked Michael enough already when he set the team record, but I liked him even more when he said afterward, "In my mind, there is never going to be another L.T. I could have 500 sacks, but there just will never be another Lawrence Taylor. Best defensive player to ever play."

Michael set the single-season sack record against the Packers in 2001. Mark Gastineau held the record with 22 in 1984 when he played for the Jets. I had a chance to break the record in 1986 when I went into the final game of the season with 20.5 sacks. We also played Green Bay, but those guys made sure I didn't get it. We won that game 55–24 and the team had like nine sacks. I didn't have a sniff.

Michael will be forever linked with Brett Favre's decision to go to the ground, which allowed Michael to break Gasteau's record. Michael has had to live with that ever since. He talked about his record on NFL Network's *A Football Life: Michael Strahan*.

"The sack record's great—absolutely phenomenal, but I almost feel like in a sense it was diminished, because everyone goes, 'Oh, Brett Favre gave you a sack.' I caught so much flak over it. It's not worth it, because everyone looks as if one sack that they question is the defining moment of my career.

"I didn't have a sack in the first three weeks of the [record-setting] season [in 2001]. So from four weeks on—13 games, 22-and-a-half sacks. That's hard to match, and I've never spoken like this about it, because I've always kind of taken it, but I always have to say, if you don't like it, then break it."

Michael retired after the 2007 season and a Super Bowl win over the Patriots. His final sack came in the third quarter of that game, when he hauled down Tom Brady. He put in 15 years in the league and he went out on top. That's the way you want to do it.

Throughout it all, he remained humble. During his induction speech at the Hall of Fame, he said: "I am an absolutely improbable Hall of Famer....I am an improbable football player."

He also paid tribute to me when he said, "One thing I can say about Lawrence Taylor is everyone knows he's a great football player, and everyone knows he's a great athlete because he watched the games. But if you watched the practices, you'd understand why. Take a scout team play, running 100 miles per hour every single play he's on that field, that's how I learned how a real pro practices. That's what I learned from you, Lawrence. But I also learned that it's okay to sleep in meetings sometimes. Even though you did it all the time. Thank you. There you go."

Michael looked at me during his speech and said: "When I was a rookie, I was scared of you. Now I'm retired and I'm up here with you with this yellow jacket, I'm still scared of you."

Looking around at some of the guys I played with, and me, too, there were some really good defensive players on the Giants. I mean Harry Carson and Carl Banks—they were really good run defenders. And me, I was a pretty good pass rusher. But Michael combined both. That's what made him a great player. I think the era when we played had better football. But I think that Strahan could have played in any era.

PHIL SIMMS

Phil Simms joined the Giants two years before I got there and he got out of the gate quickly.

Nobody knew who he was when the Giants picked him out of Morehead State University with the seventh pick of the 1979 NFL Draft. Then he won his first five starts during his rookie season and most people felt like the Giants had found their quarterback for the future.

Phil made the NFL All-Rookie Team and finished as the runner-up for the 1979 Rookie of the Year after throwing 13 touchdown passes for 1,743 yards.

But he struggled after his rookie season. He got injured a lot and didn't show much consistency when he did play.

In my rookie year, he separated his shoulder in a late-season loss to the Redskins. Scott Brunner took over at quarterback and we went to the playoffs. Phil seemed to fall further off the radar when he tore a knee ligament during a 1982 preseason game and missed all of 1982. That prompted Bill Parcells to go with Brunner when he became the new coach before the 1983 season.

But Brunner didn't fare so well during the early part of the season. When he got off to a cold start in our game against the Eagles at Giants Stadium on October 9, Parcells made a change and brought in Phil. That pleased to no end the 73,291 fans at Giants Stadium who had been chanting, "We want Simms."

The previous week Phil had demanded that the Giants trade him. And there were a lot of rumors that such a deal might come to fruition. We trailed 14–6 when he entered the game and he quickly completed four of five passes in leading the offense on a touchdown drive that culminated with Butch Woolfolk's seven-yard touchdown run.

Unfortunately, he wasn't able to finish the game.

Simms played three more plays before he hit his throwing hand on defensive tackle Dennis Harrison's helmet and came away with a compound dislocation of the thumb to end his season.

The injuries were one thing, but in my opinion the missing ingredient Phil needed to find was leadership. In his early years in the league he wasn't the leader he would become. It was a while before Phil became a leader because he always blamed everybody else. Once he became a leader, he took responsibility for his own actions. He ran that team. But it took a while.

Meanwhile, our offensive line got better and Simms began to do more film work. That allowed him to learn defenses better and gave him the ability to audible out of a play if he needed to. He also strengthened his body in the offseason.

The results began to show in 1984 when he threw for 22 touchdown passes and 4,044 yards while leading us to the playoffs.

Simms had another great season in 1985 when he threw 22 touchdowns and nearly accrued 4,000 passing yards. Included in his performances were back-to-back games when he threw for almost 1,000 yards against the Cowboys and Bengals. Unfortunately, seven turnovers were mixed in with his success and we lost both games. Still, he really seemed to come into his own that season.

By 1986 he had evolved into a complete quarterback.

He stood up strong, stopped trying to throw those 90-yard bombs, and started looking at the guy who was wide open five feet in front of him, 10 yards in front of him. He started hitting that guy and the game started to change. And he'd become a leader by then and went on from there.

Everybody on the team looked up to Phil in 1986 and we were in perfect position to make a Super Bowl run. He came through and we went 14–2 that season with him running the offense and our defense doing its thing.

When we reached the Super Bowl at the end of that season, Phil got into a zone against the Broncos, completing passes all over the place. By the time we'd finished taking care of the Broncos 39–20, he was voted the game's most valuable player after completing 22 of 25 passes. Parcells even seemed awestruck when he said of Phil's performance, "This might be the best game a quarterback has ever played."

Phil had a great season in 1990 when we returned to the Super Bowl. But his season got cut short when he broke his foot in our 15th game of the season, which came against the Bills. We ended up beating the Bills in the Super Bowl with Jeff Hostetler at quarterback.

Phil ended his career with a bang, leading us to an 11–5 record in 1993. We won our first playoff game against the Vikings before bowing out against the 49ers in a game where we got blown out. I announced my retirement after that 49ers game and, as it turned out, that ended up being Phil's last game, as well.

He had shoulder surgery after the 1993 season and was expected to return to be the team's quarterback in 1994. But somewhere along the way the Giants decided to release Phil. Dan Reeves and George Young made the call based on his salary, his shoulder, and his age. Wellington Mara did not go along with the decision, but he had always allowed Young to make all the calls—even the tough ones— and did not interfere. He did express his feelings by saying, "In this particular case, I told George that I disagree."

Rather than play for another team, he decided to retire.

I understood that the Giants cut Phil because they wanted to go another direction and there were the complications of the salary structure with the salary cap added to that. However, I do think Phil should have been able to end his career on his own terms. It wasn't bad the way he went out. I just think it could have been better.

Phil finished his career with 33,462 passing yards. And remember, those yards came during a time when the rules didn't favor the quarterback, and the offense in general, like they do now.

Phil has done well after football, finding a career in the broadcast booth. His two sons, Chris and Matt, went on to play in the NFL.

PHIL McCONKEY

Phil McConkey caught Tom Landry's attention.

The iconic Dallas Cowboys coach once said McConkey could catch a punt in a rock slide—a pretty nice compliment from a Hall of Fame coach, and a perfect description of McConkey.

Our special teams coach Romeo Crennel's first order of business for the punt return team was ball security. McConkey's ability to safely haul in any punt played into the decision to keep him when he joined the Giants in 1983. We had 120 players in camp. Of those, 14 were wide receivers. That meant one thing for those receivers: they had better be able to play special teams.

Receiving punts takes a lot of nerve. You never know if you're going to get hammered right when you catch the ball. Sometimes you might even get popped before you catch the ball. Phil had balls, which you would have expected given his background.

Phil grew up in Buffalo where his father worked as a police officer. After playing defensive back and wide receiver at Canisius High School in Buffalo—where they did not lose a game in three seasons while Phil played for the team—he earned an appointment to the U.S. Naval Academy.

Despite his lack of size, he played well for Navy as a receiver and a punt return guy. Noteworthy was his final game at Navy when he helped the Midshipmen upset BYU in the inaugural Holiday Bowl in

1978. He caught a game-winning 65-yard touchdown to earn MVP honors. Jim McMahon played quarterback for BYU.

Military service followed.

Phil served as a Navy officer and helicopter pilot for four years. Once that obligation ran its course, he began thinking about returning to the football field. That hankering led him to contact Steve Belichick, who was Navy's backfield coach. After getting a look at Phil, Belichick contacted his son, Bill, who was the Giants' defensive coordinator. That led to an opportunity with the Giants.

Thus, McConkey entered the league as a 27-year-old rookie.

If you're a long shot like Phil was, you had to have a lot of heart because he sure didn't have size, though he could run a little bit. A football team takes all kinds of guys. Sometimes I think the people who pick teams get a little carried away with their stopwatches, or with how much weight a player can lift or his size. When that's the case, you might see a football player or two slip through the cracks. Phil wasn't anything special. Phil was just a football player.

His first two seasons with the Giants he played in 29 games as a kick return/punt return man and as a receiver. Phil compiled his best statistical season in 1985, when he returned 53 punts for 442 yards, gained 234 yards returning kickoffs, and caught 25 passes for 404 yards. Still, the Giants released him prior to the 1986 season. The Packers signed him, but not for long.

We were four games into the 1986 season when one of our receivers, Lionel Manuel, hurt his knee and our punt return man, Mark Collins, suffered a concussion, which left two gaps to fill. Meanwhile, the Packers needed to create a spot on their roster for running back Eddie Lee Ivery. So the Giants traded the Packers an 11th-round draft choice for Phil, who filled both gaps. That worked out to be a good thing for Phil as well as a good thing for the Giants.

Phil brought us a lift. You need guys like him on the roster. They remind you why you love the game. Phil loved playing football. He also played well, catching 16 passes for 279 yards and making

32 returns for 253 yards. That all contributed to our 14–2 season en route to us earning a trip to Super Bowl XXI. He also became a fan favorite. He loved to wave a towel to get fans worked up into a fever before or during the game.

Phil is best remembered for the big plays he made in that Super Bowl when we beat the Broncos 39–20.

He had a 25-yard punt return that set up a field goal. Later we ran a flea flicker that saw a pass thrown his way. His 44-yard gain on that play put us at the Denver 1. Joe Morris ran it in on the next play to give us a 26–10 lead.

Finally, lady luck shined on Phil and the Giants in the fourth quarter.

We were on the Broncos' 6 when Phil Simms threw to our tight end Mark Bavaro.

Bavaro couldn't make the catch and the ball shot into the air. Phil saw the ball and went for it. Sliding on his knees, he managed to make the catch right before the ball hit the ground.

"I could see it tumbling down to me," Phil recounted to *The Buffalo News.* "Like a snowflake in the sky.... It was all white noise. I was in a cocoon—100,000 in the stands, 100 million watching on TV—and it was like I was all alone with the ball, in a dreamlike state.... All your senses are heightened in that moment. I can still remember the smell of the grass."

Phil's catch put us up 33–10 and pretty much put the game away.

Phil played two more seasons for the Giants before playing his final season in 1989 for the Chargers and the Cardinals. He finished his six-year career with 228 punt returns for 1,832 yards and 69 kick-off returns for 1,324 yards. He also hauled in 67 passes for 1,113 yards and two touchdowns. And he helped us win a Super Bowl.

Not bad for an undersized kid from Buffalo.

RODNEY HAMPTON

Rodney Hampton came to us at the perfect time, even though some were curious why we picked a running back in the first round of the 1990 NFL Draft.

At time we had four pretty good running backs on our roster: Joe Morris, Ottis Anderson, Dave Meggett, and Lewis Tillman.

Running backs were getting drafted left and right in the first round that year.

The Jets took Blair Thomas out of Penn State with the second pick of the draft. They would regret that one. Emmitt Smith (17th), Darrell Thompson (19th), and Steve Broussard (20th pick) were also picked before the Giants used the 24th pick to get Rodney.

Obviously, Smith became a star, accruing more yards, touchdowns, and carries than any player before him. The others picked prior to Rodney didn't turn out that well, though.

Rodney had been a star at Georgia. He had good size at 6'0", 215 pounds, could bang, and had quickness. He just wasn't the fastest guy on the board, which is probably why we were able to get him when we did. The big question facing the Giants was whether they felt like Rodney could give them more than Dexter Carter, who didn't have much size, but had speed. As usual, George Young did his homework, saw something in Rodney other teams didn't see, and picked him when he had the chance.

I think the decision came down to the fact that we played in the NFC East. Would you rather have a guy who could hit the line and get you the hard yards, really stick his nose in there? Or would you rather have the speedster who might get slowed down in the weather we played in or easily injured because of the style our offense played?

Rodney didn't miss a beat making the transition from the SEC to the NFL.

He caught everybody's attention with his first professional carry in a preseason game against the Bills at Buffalo. In the second quarter of that game, he took a handoff on a draw play and didn't stop running until 89 yards later after he went into the end zone. Along the way, he left a linebacker's jock behind him, broke a tackle, and outraced everybody to the end zone. But he didn't have much speed, right?

Anderson got most of the carries for us, but Rodney played in 15 games his rookie season, started two games, and rushed for 455 yards and two touchdowns. He also caught 32 passes for another 274 yards and two touchdowns. Having O.J. Anderson and Rodney Hampton— hey, one is off and hopefully the other one isn't off. That would be a big plus for any offense.

Unfortunately, on January 13, 1991, Rodney got hurt when we were playing the Bears in New York in a divisional playoff game. Hostetler got sacked by Steve McMichael in the second quarter and Hostetler fumbled. Rodney tried to recover the ball. Somebody got him from behind and he hurt his leg. He knew he was hurt, but he stayed in one more play before he left the game. Turned out he had a broken leg, and he was finished for the season.

Ottis took over after that. This is where having Rodney during the season was important. Ottis turned 34 at the end of that season and was the oldest back in the league. By the start of our playoff run he had played 12 seasons in the league and had 2,500 regular season and playoff carries. He could still get the job done, but he could no longer put an offense on his back and carry it for a season. Since Rodney had been sharing the load, Ottis was fresher than he otherwise would have been that late in the season. Of course Ottis went on to be the man for us in the playoffs and ended up being the Super Bowl MVP when we beat the Bills in Tampa.

After Rodney's rookie season, he broke 1,000 yards the next five seasons, so I saw him have a lot of good games before I retired after the 1993 season. Probably one of the best came in our Wild Card game against the Vikings on January 9, 1994.

We had brutal weather for that one. Phil Simms couldn't get anything going throwing the ball because of the wind and they were beating us 10–3 at the half. Fortunately, Rodney wasn't affected by the wind. In our first possession of the second half, he took off for a 51-yard touchdown run that included a wicked stiff arm to linebacker Carlos Jenkins. He basically did it all that day, running the ball 33 times for 161 yards and two touchdowns in our 17–10 win. That game meant a lot to me, because I knew it was my last at Giants Stadium.

Rodney made the Pro Bowl in 1992 and 1993 and gained 6,897 career rushing yards, which were the most yards in team history until Tiki Barber broke his record in 2004. The Giants released him prior to the 1998 season and he said he wasn't ready to retire just yet. Several teams were said to be interested in him, but he ended up retiring, meaning he spent his entire career with the Giants.

JUMBO ELLIOTT

You don't get a nickname like "Jumbo" unless you fit the bill. John Stuart "Jumbo" Elliott fit the bill and more.

Jumbo came to us in the second round of the 1988 Draft out of the University of Michigan, all 6'7", 310 pounds of him—a big boy and the perfect guy to play left tackle in our offense. You always want a guy like that protecting your quarterback's back.

Jumbo played for the Giants from 1988 to 1995 and none of those eight seasons was bigger than the 1990 season.

We got a pretty good idea about how much better of a team we were with Jumbo when he missed eight games with a broken bone in his left leg during the middle of that season. With Jumbo in the lineup, the offense averaged almost 150 rushing yards a game. Without him, we were at about 110.

Leading us into Super Bowl XXV, Jumbo pancaked the likes of Minnesota's Chris Doleman, Buffalo's Bruce Smith, Arizona's Ken Harvey, New England's Andre Tippett, Chicago's Richard Dent, and San Francisco's Kevin Fagan. Add those guys up and you've taken care of business against a pretty impressive group of opponents. Jumbo just dominated them.

He continued to dominate in the Super Bowl when we beat the Bills.

Controlling the football was a big part of our game plan in Super

Bowl XXV. The way he controlled Bruce Smith helped us win that game.

We ran 73 plays on offense and rushed for 172 yards. That allowed us to keep the ball for 40 minutes. Ottis Anderson got 102 yards on the ground in that game and most of those yards came while running behind Jumbo.

The offense kept the ball a long, long time, converting on 9-of-16 third-down situations. And we knew once we got ahead, our guys were going to run the tar out of the ball. Having Jumbo on our side really helped that pursuit.

Sometimes a little extra motivation would be used to help Jumbo.

Don't get me wrong, Jumbo could do it all. He was big enough and strong enough to take care of business. But every now and then a challenge would come along. The NFL has a way of presenting challenges. Bill Parcells could see the challenges coming. That's when he'd put me up against Jumbo in practice.

I used to like going against him. And Bill would always put me against him when he was trying to get Jumbo ready. Like when he had somebody like a Bruce Smith to go against in the Super Bowl. Then I was going to work against him in all the practices leading up to that game. I would work Jumbo all week and just try to frustrate him. When Jumbo got frustrated, he would come back on Sunday and the poor guy he lined up against would get his ass kicked. That guy was a fighter.

When Parcells wanted me to give him some work, I knew what he wanted me to do and why.

Jumbo had trouble with quickness. If somebody got on him real quick and made moves on him, he had trouble with that. Anybody who wanted to try and power rush Jumbo Elliot was stupid because he had trees for arms. But you had to move him.

Going against him, I would never, ever do a straight rush. I would go inside him, outside him, do a spin, just to get him better. And from where he was his first year to where he ended up in his career was amazing. The guy became a phenomenal player.

Before Super Bowl XXV, Parcells knew stopping Smith would be key. Smith was All-Pro every year and just a different kind of player. He could get after the quarterback but he was strong enough to do well against the run, too. Jumbo had his work cut out for him, because Smith was a complete player. Given the fact Smith was so good Parcells had no other choice but to put me in there against Jumbo during practice.

It was so funny, because the No. 1s never go against the No. 1s. Your No. 1 defense doesn't go against your No. 1 offense. Usually that doesn't happen in practice. That will happen during the preseason, but not during the regular season. But that whole week before we played Buffalo, I worked Jumbo—just Jumbo. Anytime he was in there, I got out there. I worked him all week and I got him pissed. All week long he was cussing and he was fighting. But I'll tell you what— he kicked ass on that Sunday. He kicked ass. What a job he put on. It was just great to see.

Jumbo had his days, and games, where you couldn't make him any better. But you get him on the right day and motivate him enough and you talk enough junk to him, and Jumbo Elliott could be even more of a force to reckon with.

Jumbo moved on to the Jets in 1996, signing a five-year deal as a free agent. He retired in 2002.

Funny thing, as good of a player as Jumbo was, he's probably best remembered for a game that took place on October 23, 2000. By then he wasn't even starting for the Jets, but the play everybody remembers took place on a special night when the Jets beat the Dolphins 40–37 in an overtime win that came to be known as the "Monday Night Miracle."

In that game, the Jets trailed 30–7 in the fourth quarter, but they never quit.

Vinny Testaverde threw five touchdown passes in the game and one of them went to Jumbo, who bobbled the ball before hauling in the three-yard touchdown pass while falling down in the end zone. Jumbo's first, and only, catch tied the game at 37 to send it into overtime.

Pretty nice moment for Jumbo, but remember, this guy wasn't a pass receiver. Offensive tackle was his trade and he was one of the best.

JEFF HOSTETLER

Jeff Hostetler never got the respect he probably deserved; he just got the job done.

If you looked back at his career, you could see how he developed the tough skin he needed to handle adversity. That tough skin and his unique skills ended up helping us win our second Super Bowl in 1991.

At Penn State, Hostetler earned the starting quarterback job in 1980 and started the first three games of the season before losing the job to Todd Blackledge. That prompted him to transfer to West Virginia, where he sat out the 1981 season due to NCAA transfer rules. He then started in 1982 and 1983, winning some big games along the way and earning the love of West Virginia fans, which inspired a record, "Ole Hoss (The Ballad of West Virginia's Jeff Hostetler)."

By the time he left West Virginia, he had led the Mountaineers to two bowl games and an 18–6 mark. Hostetler didn't have a big arm, but he brought a different element to the game because he was mobile. That different dimension enticed the Giants to draft him in the third round of the 1984 NFL Draft.

He spent the next five seasons living the charmed life of a quarterback holding a clipboard on the sideline while Phil Simms got all the action.

Hostetler did not get his first start until November 27, 1988, when we played the Saints in New Orleans. He led us to a 13–12 win that day. He started for us again the next season and he helped us win a game against the Vikings. Still, Hostetler didn't appear to be anything special. For the most part, his main function was to play late in lopsided games.

Like most backups, Hostetler got frustrated with his situation. He even volunteered to play other positions. Fate finally intervened late in the 1990 season when Simms suffered a season-ending foot injury.

Phil had a tremendous year going. But Phil getting hurt might have been the best thing that happened to the New York Giants that year.

A lot of the experts counted us out, but Hostetler stepped right in and brought us something different. He could run the football. Third-and-4, he could take off. Nobody else was ready for that.

He led us to wins in our final two regular season games and our two playoff games against the Bears and the 49ers.

Hostetler sucked it up against the 49ers in the NFC Championship game when he injured his knee and had to leave the game. He came back in to lead two scoring drives in our 15–13 win.

In Super Bowl XXV he completed 20 of 32 passes for 222 yards against the Bills and we came away with a 20–19 win.

Looking back at that 1990 season, Simms was having a great year before getting injured. We weren't the best team in the league, particularly after Simms went down and Hostetler came in. There were three or four teams better than us. But I credit Hostetler for getting us to that Super Bowl.

We'd lost one of the league's best passers. Hostetler wasn't going to kill you with his arm, but he would kill you with his feet. People weren't used to that with us, having a quarterback that's going to scramble around. Instead of throwing for that five-yard first down, he'd tuck the ball and run. I think if it wasn't for Hostetler being able to pick up those yards when everybody was covered, we wouldn't have gotten to that Super Bowl. He really shouldered a load.

Bill Parcells retired after we won the Super Bowl and Ray Handley took over as our coach. One of his calls was to let Hostetler compete against Simms going into the next season. Unexpectedly, he won the job and started twelve games for us before breaking his back.

Simms beat him out the next season and held the job until he experienced yet another season-ending injury. That made Hostetler our starter again until he got injured.

Even though Hostetler had the best record of any Giants starting quarterback in 1992 at 5–4, our new coach in 1993, Dan Reeves, opted to go with Simms. Hostetler signed with the Los Angeles Raiders to be their starter in 1993 and spent four seasons there.

During his tenure with the Raiders, he threw for 294 yards and three touchdowns in a 42–24 playoff win over the Denver Broncos in the 1993 season. He got voted to his only Pro Bowl in 1994. He moved on to finish his career with the Redskins, when he started three games in 1997.

Overall, Hostetler had a pretty nice career. He completed 1,357 of 2,338 passes attempted for 16,430 yards and 94 touchdowns. He also ran for 1,391 yards and 17 touchdowns.

Again, Hostetler wasn't the fancy sports car, he was the 4x4 truck. He brought a little something different to the offense. At the end of the day I think his playoff record speaks volumes. Some guys don't play as well when the game has added importance. He proved that he was just the opposite. Hostetler played in five playoff games in his career and connected on 72 of 115 passes for 1,034 yards, seven touchdowns, and no interceptions. That's money.

THE SUBURBANITES

A composite character of "the Suburbanites" looked like the accountant who was married with kids and lived in a nice three-two on a cul-de-sac just outside the city.

But looks could be deceiving. Those sonsofbitches could block.

"The Suburbanites" were composed of guards Bill Ard and Chris Godfrey, center Bart Oates, and tackles Karl Nelson and Brad Benson. They seemed like they were all the same guy: young white guys with wives and children, the kind of guys who would have you over to their houses for a few beers while they cooked burgers on a charcoal grill.

Bill Parcells gave the group their nickname that stuck and he had a lot of fun at the group's expense along the way. Godfrey explained to Giants.com the rationale behind Parcells' humor.

"Parcells shot a lot of jibes at us and one of them was that we all looked like guys that mom drove to practice," Godfrey said. "We all had responsible offseason jobs and families out in the suburbs, and he was relentless with his little digs."

Oates told the *Chicago Tribune*: "We all live at least a 30-minute drive from [Giants Stadium]. We're just everyday suburban guys."

And Benson said of the group: "Okay, maybe it isn't a nickname a motorcycle gang would have picked out, but it fits us pretty well. The other guys gave it to us and we haven't been able to talk our way out of it. Before it was the Suburbanites, some of the defensive players were calling us the Attaché Cases, because a few of us carry them to practice every day."

All five of "the Suburbanites" were married and they all lived in Jersey suburbs. They weren't your typical NFL players. Nelson was a mechanical engineer. Oates went to Brigham Young and had been a two-time academic All-American. Ard worked as a stockbroker in the offseason. Benson once ran a guard-dog business, and Godfrey was a free-thinking philosopher of sorts.

When Parcells wasn't poking fun at them, he praised them by saying: "They work together, and they have a good work ethic."

"The Suburbanites" protected Phil Simms and blocked for Joe Morris. The way they went about their business in 1985 played a large role in us going 10–6 that season. You have to be able to play smash-mouth football in the NFC East, and they fit that mold perfectly.

Everybody made a big deal about "the Suburbanites" facing "the Monsters of the Midway" when we played in the Bears in the 1986 playoffs. That one didn't turn out well for us, but the next season they paved the way for our Super Bowl run and they kicked ass in the Super Bowl against the Broncos.

Those guys played together well. They were cohesive and a real unit. They came off the ball and they didn't make mental mistakes. "The Suburbanites" were a hell of a unit. I don't think there was a better offensive line there when they played. And, of course, they loved their nickname. As Godfrey once said: "When you call yourselves the Suburbanites, it's not much to live up to."

JOE MORRIS

Joe Morris was a very tough guy. But it took him a while to become that breakout player.

The Giants drafted him in the second round of the 1982 Draft, the year after I got drafted. We took Butch Woolfolk in the first round of the same draft, so you had to figure Woolfolk would get the better shot. But like I said, Joe was a tough guy. He had to be tough because he only stood about five-foot-nothing.

Growing up, I'm sure his size always put a chip on Morris' shoulder. Everybody underestimates the little guy. But he put numbers on the board.

Just look at what he did at Syracuse, where he started for four years. By the time he made his last carry, he'd set all the school's rushing records. And we're talking about some football royalty that he passed—Jim Brown, Larry Csonka, and Floyd Little.

Joe scored a touchdown in his first professional run and battled Woolfolk for the job until the 1984 season. Woolfolk got hurt and Bill Parcells told Joe to get into the backfield and stay there until he told him otherwise. That didn't mean he wouldn't have more competition.

First they signed free agent Maurice Carthon, who had played for the New Jersey Generals, and then they selected George Adams of Kentucky on the first round of the NFL draft.

Parcells sounded like he loved Adams and planned on using the

6'1", 225-pounder in goal-line and short-yardage situations. Parcells said Adams was "big, strong, and durable, and he can run quite a bit, block, and catch the ball." And he was "a lunch-pail guy in attitude."

Joe wasn't about to let Adams win the job. That was the year Joe really established himself, running for 1,336 yards and 21 touchdowns. That same season, he ran for 141 yards in our 17–3 win over the 49ers in the playoffs.

Adams never really panned out.

I think everything began to change for Joe when he learned how to pick up his feet. Before that, Joe could trip over a Tic Tac. Picking up his feet made all the difference.

He went over 1,000 yards the next season, too.

We played power football. If you play up in the Northeast you had to because you were always playing in bad weather. That kind of football suited Joe.

When we went on our Super Bowl run in 1986, he gained 159 yards against the 49ers in our first playoff game. One of those was a 45-yard touchdown romp and he also scored from two yards out to put the icing on the 49–3 win. The next week he ran for 86 yards and scored another touchdown when we beat the Redskins 17–0 to earn a trip to the Super Bowl.

Phil Simms stole the show at the Super Bowl that year, but Joe again played a big role. He ran for 67 yards and scored a touchdown. He also took part in what turned out to be a back-breaking play for the Broncos' fortunes that nobody saw coming, including most of our team.

Throughout the season, Parcells had the offense run a razzle-dazzle, flea-flicker play in practice that he never called in the games. Joe, like most of the offense, had grown tired of the play and they constantly complained about why they continued to practice a play they never ran. Then Parcells goes and calls the play in the third quarter of the biggest game we'd ever played. Even Simms couldn't believe that he'd called the play, because he stepped out of the huddle to look at

Bill like, *What the hell?* Parcells told him to run the damn play.

And they did.

Joe took the handoff from Simms then tossed the ball back to Simms, who threw a 44-yard strike to Phil McConkey that took us to the 1-yard line. Joe ran it in on the next play to give us a 26–10 lead and we cruised from there.

Joe ran for 1,741 yards the next two seasons before an injury caused him to miss all of 1989. When he returned in 1990, Rodney Hampton beat him out of the job and the Giants released him. He played one more season with the Browns in 1991 before retiring.

Joe compiled an impressive body of work in seven seasons with us. From 1982 through 1988, he gained 5,585 yards while averaging 4.0 yards a carry and scoring 48 touchdowns.

Joe used to run the cutback play to perfection. I'll bet you he made 50 percent of his yards on that one play, that little cutback. I'll tell you what, I'll bet you 50 or 60 percent of his yardage came off that one play because he could run it better than anybody in the league.

THE NFC EAST

Playing in the NFC East brought a challenge every season. We had no doubt in our minds we were playing in the best division in the NFL.

Throughout my career, the Giants were in the NFC East along with the Philadelphia Eagles, Dallas Cowboys, Washington Redskins, and St. Louis Cardinals. The Cardinals remained in our division even after they moved to Arizona following the 1987 season. They finally moved to the NFC West in 2002 when the NFL realigned to four divisions in each conference.

The Redskins played at RFK Stadium, the Eagles at Veterans Stadium, the Cowboys at Texas Stadium, and the Cardinals at Busch Stadium. All of those places brought the home team a decided advantage.

Take playing at RFK: that place had been one of the first multi-purpose stadiums. The Washington Senators played there before they moved to Arlington, Texas, and became the Texas Rangers. RFK Stadium hosted the Redskins for 36 seasons, from 1961 through 1996, which covered the length of my career. When things started to get exciting, the fans would get into it and the stands would start to shake. All of those places had loud fans. At Giants Stadium we felt like we had an advantage because of our fans in the Meadowlands.

Cardinals fans might have been the exception. You could

understand their lack of enthusiasm a little bit, since their team pretty much existed as the doormat of the division every year. They were the only team in the NFC East that did not win a division title during my career.

Teams in the division had really good talent on both sides of the ball.

Philadelphia had Randall Cunningham, Cris Carter, Keith Byars, Jerome Brown, Reggie White, Ron Jaworski, Jerry Sisemore, and Clyde Simmons. The Cowboys had Danny White, Drew Pearson, Ron Springs, Tony Dorsett, Doug Cosbie, Tony Hill, Billy Joe DuPree, Butch Johnson, Charlie Waters, D.D. Lewis, Everson Walls, Harvey Martin, Too Tall Jones, and Randy White. The Redskins had Joe Theismann, Joe Washington, Art Monk, Russ Grimm, Joe Jacoby, Dexter Manley, Joe Lavender, John Riggins, and Mark Murphy. Like I said, even the Cardinals had talent with Jim Hart, Ottis Anderson, Pat Tilley, Dan Dierdorf, E.J. Junior, Roger Wehrli, and Neil Lomax.

As for coaches, Bill Parcells wasn't the only great one in that division. Joe Gibbs coached the Redskins, Dick Vermeil the Eagles, and Tom Landry the Cowboys.

All told, we'd play eight total games a year against our NFC East opponents. Not that you would ever take any games for granted—in fact, you paid particular attention when you were playing against one of your division rivals. A lot of bad blood would circulate in those games. That's going to happen the more often you play against a certain team—or teams. Those games also created an atmosphere you enjoyed playing in. Of those teams, the Redskins were our biggest rivals.

We would play hard against each other. Sometimes there was a little bad blood, but we respected those guys and I think they respected us. We always hit hard, but the games were clean. You didn't see any cheap shots.

NFC East teams were built to play power football by necessity. You couldn't exactly air out the football in the middle of November or

December at one of the frozen venues we played in. So most teams in our division concentrated on having a power running game they could count on, with some horses up front to open the holes for pile-driving running backs. I mean, you just knew you were going to be sore the next day after playing the Redskins and looking at John Riggins all day running behind "the Hogs," as they called their front line.

All of those Hogs could play. Among that group, Russ Grimm and Joe Jacoby anchored the line.

Jacoby was a very tough player and the kind of guy you typically played against in the NFC East. I had a lot of battles on Sunday against that guy. He stood 6'7", about 300 pounds, but he could move a little bit. He could hold his own against me even though I was more athletic. I knew I couldn't outmuscle Jacoby, so I'd try and get him to put his hands up too early. Once he did that, I could get past him and zero in on their quarterback.

Still, for somebody his size he could pull on the Redskins' counter-trey running play. You certainly couldn't overpower him. You had to hope you could get him moving a little bit, because if he got his hands on you that was all she wrote.

Most of the stadiums in our division had artificial surfaces, so that would take its toll on your body, too. Back then the artificial stuff we played on felt like playing on concrete.

You knew the teams you were playing against in your division were the teams you were competing against for a playoff spot. That made it more of a rivalry. I mean, it felt like college football rivals.

We you play teams twice in a season, it's tough to sweep a team. We swept the Redskins during the 1986 season en route to the playoffs where we met them again in the NFC Conference Championship. I'm sure there were a lot of people who didn't think we could beat them a third time, and normally that would have been a pretty good bet. But the wind was whipping around something fierce that day. The wind chill was in the 20s. Once Parcells saw the flags blowing straight out, he decided after winning the toss to kick off. That turned out to be a wise decision. We scored 10 points in the first quarter and it felt like the game was already over.

As for all of those teams, I probably got up a little bit more for the Redskins because my dad had been a Redskins fan growing up in Virginia.

Survival of the fittest definitely took place every year in the NFC East. So if you finished at the top of our division, you were trained to beat the best. You had a good chance of doing well in the postseason because of what you'd been through during the season. In my 13 years in the league, seven NFC East teams reached the Super Bowl, and they went 5–2 in those games. That's a pretty impressive stat, but not really surprising when you consider what the teams in the NFC East went through back then.

Dan Reeves

I embraced Dan Reeves' arrival when he became the Giants' head coach in 1993.

At the time the Giants hired him, I wasn't sure if 1993 would be my final season or if I'd already played my final season in 1992. Everything began to click once the Giants changed coaches, though.

They brought in Reeves to replace Ray Handley.

Reeves had been in the league a long time.

He'd been a running back and played eight seasons with the Cowboys. Among the highlights of his days playing under Tom Landry was the touchdown pass he threw when the Cowboys lost to the Packers in the NFL Championship Game, which came to be known as the "Ice Bowl."

Reeves' resume showed a winner. The Cowboys teams he played for made the playoffs every year of his career—which was a lot harder to do back in the day when there were fewer spots. He went to two Super Bowls and was part of the winning team that defeated the Dolphins 24–3 in Super Bowl VI following the 1971 season.

When he became the Broncos' head coach in 1981, he ranked as the youngest coach in the league. His excellence continued as a coach. So I wanted to come back from my Achilles injury and play for the guy. Be a part of his program. The guy knew how to win. He'd always known how to win. I put him up there with Bill Parcells. I respected the man. So I decided to give it a go. I totally bought into what Reeves was selling.

I liked the new defensive coordinator, Mike Nolan, over Rod Rust, who had a "read and react" scheme that none of us liked. Mike reminded me of Belichick when he had been a young man and our defensive coordinator. I also like the fact that Reeves went with Phil Simms as our starting quarterback. Jeff Hostetler went to Oakland as a free agent and we no longer had a quarterback controversy. I always thought Phil needed to be our starter. You couldn't replace how smart he was on the field.

Reeves got a little ticked about how in the past I'd never gone to the minicamps or didn't report to training camp on time. He told the papers, "I know how Lawrence has felt about these things in the past. But this is the future now. I don't know of anyone ever [rehabilitating] the Achilles on the golf course."

I didn't mind that Reeves did that. Our team had kind of strayed from the way we'd been after Parcells left. We weren't as dedicated. I think using me as an example helped show the team he wasn't messing around.

Reeves had coached the Broncos for 12 seasons. Along the way, he took the team to three Super Bowls—all of which they lost—in advance of having differences with the team's star quarterback, John Elway. Elway won that battle and Reeves got sent packing. Ironically, he wasn't the Giants' first pick. They tried to hire Dave Wannstedt and Tom Coughlin before offering the job to Reeves.

Reeves came in and wasn't wishy-washy in the least about his intentions. He wasn't afraid to make changes. One of the first moves he made was to end the quarterback controversy by releasing Hoss. That took some balls since Phil was 38 at the time and had missed the final 12 games of the 1992 season due to elbow surgery.

Phil went on to start all 16 games. Reeves also revamped the offense and brought Broncos players to the team. He cut Pepper Johnson, who had started every game the previous three seasons and had been a Pro Bowl linebacker. That left a linebacker corps of me, Carlton Bailey, Corey Miller, and Michael Brooks. We also had Marcus Buckley, Kanavis McGhee, and Jessie Armstead. Matt Bahr and Sean Landeta, our kicker and punter, respectively, also got sent packing. None of those were easy calls based on how much they had contributed to our past success. And it took somebody like Reeves to make those decisions.

Everybody worked hard for Dan. I liked playing for a coach that I felt had control of the team. He meant business and he created a professional and energetic atmosphere. Basically he brought in a better discipline than we'd had in the previous years. Guys respected him as a person and a coach and he was a fair guy. All of that felt refreshing after the previous year when things got out of hand.

The guy was thorough, too. He always concentrated on the little things. That made you concentrate on the little things, too. For example, he set up a 40-second clock on the sideline to make sure our offense got off the snap in time to meet a new NFL time limit for getting off plays.

During preseason training camp he held single practices on Wednesdays and Saturdays instead of doubles on those days. I think that made everybody work harder when they were at practice and made for crisper practices and a better atmosphere in camp.

We ended up going 11–5 in 1993, which got us a Wild Card spot in the playoffs. We beat Minnesota in our Wild Card game before losing to San Francisco the next week to end our season and end my career.

When the Giants went 5–11 in 1995 and then 6–10 in 1996, Reeves got fired. He went on to coach the Falcons and led that franchise to their best-ever season, when they went to the Super Bowl in 1998. Ironically, they lost to the Broncos.

GIANTS STADIUM

Giants Stadium served as the home of the Giants for the length of my career.

I always loved the energy at that place. The fans were great. And we felt like we had a decided home-field advantage whenever we played there.

There wasn't anything really distinctive about Giants Stadium other than the weather. Opposing teams hated playing there, mostly because of the weather.

Quarterbacks couldn't stand the thought of throwing the football there. Punters and kickers probably hated the place even more. Giants Stadium acquired the nickname "the Swamp" because it was built in the Jersey Meadowlands in the middle of a location that had been a swamp. Former Atlanta Falcons defensive end Tim Green came up with another name for the place. In his book, *The Dark Side of the Game: My Life in the NFL*, he wrote the following passage about Giants Stadium: "Football in a tin can. Curse the Giants for ever leaving Yankee Stadium." (I've called the place the "Tin Can" ever since.)

They built Giants Stadium for $78 million. Prior to the opening of the place that was located in East Rutherford, New Jersey, in the Meadowlands Sports complex, the Giants played at Yankee Stadium until 1972. The team then played two years at the Yale Bowl in New Haven, Connecticut, before they played the 1975 season at Shea

Stadium.

Finally, on October 10, 1976, the Giants officially moved into Giants Stadium, an 80,242-capacity stadium owned and operated by the New Jersey Sports and Exposition Authority. The Giants had played their first four games of the season on the road before hosting the Cowboys that day with 76,042 watching the Cowboys take a 24–14 win.

The Jets became Giants Stadium's second tenant in 1984.

Hosting two teams allowed Giants Stadium to break the record established by Chicago's Wrigley Field for most NFL games played at any stadium, which had been 365. Giants Stadium broke that record during the Jets' 2003 home opener against the Dolphins.

My first game at Giants Stadium took place in our 1981 season opener on September 6 against the Eagles. We lost that one 24–10. We heard a lot of boos that day, too.

Of course, Giants fans had seen a lot of losing to that point. The previous five years had seen the Giants go just 24–52, so the start of 1981 looked like more of the same.

Billy Taylor got booed by the 71,459 in attendance when he fumbled at the end of the first half to set up an Eagles field goal. Then they booed when we went three and out the second time we had the ball in the second half. The announcement of free Giants football calendars got booed and finally, Beasley Reece got booed off the field when he got burned by a 55-yard touchdown pass from Ron Jaworski to Rodney Parker.

You understood the fans' frustration. I thought the boos at least showed that the fans cared. That climate at my first game contrasted dramatically to the climate that would define Giants Stadium during my career.

My final game at Giants Stadium came on January 9, 1994, when we hosted the Vikings in a Wild Card playoff game. That game served up the perfect setting for my final game there. The temperature dipped to minus-5 degrees with the wind-chill factor caused by 26 mph winds. That's January football at Giants Stadium.

You knew when you suited up in January, you'd better be ready to play hard-nosed defense because both teams are going to bring their power games.

We beat the Vikings 17–10 that day, winning the power game as Rodney Hampton rushed for 161 yards and two touchdowns.

We got after Jim McMahon that day, too. He got hammered. They were all clean hits, but he took a beating. I actually felt sorry for him. On the other hand, I felt really good because we dominated on defense. Giants Stadium was our house and we wanted to control that game. We did.

At the end of the game, I got to hear the chants one final time: "L.T.! L.T.!" That was nice.

I don't know if I can really name my favorite game at Giants Stadium. We kicked a lot of ass in that place. Here are a few memorable ones, though.

On January 11, 1987, we hosted the NFC Championship Game and we beat the Redskins 17–0 to put us into the Super Bowl against Denver. Man, the wind was swirling that day, trash was going all over the place. And we were headed to Pasadena.

After the game we ran off through the west end zone, which was the place where Jimmy Hoffa was supposed to have been buried.

That same season Eagles coach Buddy Ryan decided that he could use his fullback, Keith Byars, to block me in our October 12 meeting. I had a pretty good day, sacking Jaworski three times in our 35–3 win.

Another game that stands out is when we knocked the 49ers out of the playoffs in 1985. We'd never won a playoff game at Giants Stadium, so there was a lot of excitement there that day.

Perhaps the single most memorable play in Giants Stadium history happened before I arrived. On November 19, 1978, the "Miracle at the Meadowlands" took place and that game did not have a happy ending for the Giants.

The Giants had the game in hand. They only needed to take a knee to finish off the game for a win against the Eagles. But for some reason, Giants quarterback Joe Pisarcik handed off to Larry Csonka, or shall we say tried to hand off. That resulted in a fumble that Herm Edwards grabbed and ran in for a game-winning touchdown.

The Giants fired their offensive coordinator Bob Gibson the next day. And John McVay, the Giants' coach, got fired at the end of that 6–10 season.

One of the odder things that occurred in the 1980s involved multiple instances of cancer in Giants players. Four Giants players in seven years got diagnosed with cancer, and two of them died: John Tuggle and Doug Kotar. That prompted a study to see if a link could be found between the cases of cancer and Giants Stadium. Once the study took place, they concluded no connection existed between Giants Stadium and cancer.

Giants Stadium shut down after the 2009 NFL season and the Giants and Jets moved to MetLife Stadium. The final game saw the Jets host the Bengals on January 3, 2010. A month later, they began tearing down the old place, a destruction that took many great football memories with it.

JOE THEISMANN'S LEG

J oe Theismann and I are linked forever because of an unfortunate
incident that happened on November 18, 1985, during a Monday
night game at RFK Stadium in Washington, D.C., against the
Redskins.

At the beginning of the second quarter, Theismann handed off to
John Riggins. The Diesel bulled toward the middle of the line, putting his head down for the impact. Then he changed his tack, stopping and flipping the ball back to Theismann. They were trying a flea
flicker. Theismann wanted to throw downfield to Art Monk.

Unfortunately for the Redskins and Theismann, we read the play
correctly. We were blitzing. It felt like our entire defense was pour-
ing in on Theismann. I got a hold of him and pulled him down. As
we went to the ground, my knee rammed into his lower right leg;
Harry Carson and Gary Reasons also congregated at Theismann on
the sack. He didn't get up. I didn't expect him to, either. I knew he'd
been hurt badly.

Theismann later told the *New York Times* in a 2005 interview: "The
pain was unbelievable, it snapped like a breadstick. It sounded like
two muzzled gunshots off my left shoulder. Pow, pow! It was at that
point, I also found out what a magnificent machine the human body
is. Almost immediately, from the knee down, all the feeling was gone

in my right leg. The endorphins had kicked in, and I was not in pain."

Everybody on the field saw Theismann sprawled out on the field and knew he was in trouble. I know I started hollering for the doctors to get to him in a hurry to give him some help. Initially, some of the Redskins thought I was taunting after the sack. That obviously wasn't the case.

It's just one of those things that happened. I knew he was hurt when I heard him under the pile yelling and I understood. That's why I tried to get everybody off him and get some help for him. I knew when you're sitting on the bottom of the pile—I don't care if it's a toe sprain, or an ankle sprain, I don't care what it is. It seems like forever, like the people on top of you are never going to figure it out. All you want is the people to get off of you and to get some help. And to breathe again.

Everybody just kind of stood around like nobody knew what had happened.

At that juncture of his career, Theismann was still a decent football player and an icon in Washington. Of course, I'd been playing against him for years. And during our time we spent a lot of time together and we'd see each other a lot. Just like anybody else, you hate to see somebody sit there and suffer. So I wanted to get some help out there for the sumbitch.

What happened? He fractured both the tibia and the fibula. In other words, the lower leg bones in his right leg were broken between his ankle and knee. That end result left his leg bent gruesomely in different directions.

A lot of time passed before they quit tending to Joe and got him off the field and on his way to the hospital. Jay Schroeder took over at quarterback. Nobody knew at the time that Theismann would never play again.

An ESPN poll of viewers later voted that play as the NFL's "Most Shocking Moment in History."

Really, it's not a moment I want to remember or care to see again. I've never seen the play. Football is a tough game, so players are always going to get hurt while playing the game. That's one of the hazards of the job. Believe me; I've seen a lot worse hits on film than the one on Joe, though. Everyone who thinks they know me wants to talk about that *Monday Night Football* game. First of all, like I said, I have never watched the play, don't won't to watch it, and I never will watch it. I saw it in person. I don't want to see it again.

I remember calling him the morning after I broke his leg. A woman answered the phone. I don't know if she was his girlfriend or wife at the time. I hear her say, "Joe, Joe, that guy is on the phone!" When he got on the phone, he told me that I had broken both the bones in his leg. I kidded him by telling him that I didn't do anything half-assed. I told him, "If I'm going to break them, I'm going to break them both."

To Joe's credit, he never blamed me for what happened. We've never had a problem. I've never had a problem with Joe. And every time we see each other we talk. We talked before then, we still talk, and there is no animosity there. I know his son very well. Hey, I did him a favor. He had Lloyd's of London. He made about $3 million.

According to a lot of people who talk about the history of the league, that play changed the left tackle position forever. Talented left tackles became a more valued commodity because the left tackle protected the quarterback's back, or blind side.

That became a critical element of Michael Lewis' book *The Blind Side*. Later, that book became a movie that starred Sandra Bullock and Tim McGraw.

The way I look at what happened and what happened as a result, I think, it is what it is. Back in those days, if you couldn't protect the backside you had a mess to clean up. Listen, somebody was going to get killed if you couldn't protect the backside. Now there is a lot more emphasis on protecting that back side. It's not a problem anymore. Offenses are swinging people that way.

Today, the back side probably has the best athletes on any team's roster. Like the movie said, you've got to protect the blind side of the quarterback. You've got to.

Joe had a helluva a career and he did well after the NFL. But he's always maintained that his legacy is that injury. As he told the *Orlando Sentinel,* "I'll forever be known as the Godfather of Broken Legs."

MVP SEASON

Defensive players don't win the Most Valuable Player Award very often, which made that accomplishment a special one for me when I won the thing in 1986.

Minnesota's Alan Page had won the award in 1971 and had been the only other defensive player to do so when I won it in 1986. Sportswriters and broadcasters from all of the NFL cities—28 at the time—gave me 41 votes to Rams running back Eric Dickerson's 17 and Dolphins quarterback Dan Marino's nine.

My 20.5 sacks worked as the sexy drawing card to entice voters to vote for me. While winning the award was special, something about winning the award almost didn't seem right, since football is such a team sport. No individual is better than the team. Individual players can't accomplish anything without players around them.

So when anybody asks me about what I did differently to win an MVP Award in 1986, I look to the team. And while doing that, I have to go back to the previous season.

We went 10–6 in 1985 and made the playoffs.

In our Wild Card game, we hosted the 49ers at Giants Stadium. Even though the 49ers hung 362 yards of total offense on us—Dwight Clark was on fire that day, catching eight passes for 120 yards—we limited the damage, holding them to one field goal. That worked for us since Joe Morris ran for 141 yards to lead our offense, and we came away 17–3 winners.

The following week we traveled to Chicago to play the Bears at Soldier Field. The Bears lost just once that season and had the look of one of the great teams in NFL history. Buddy Ryan coached the defense and they were dominant.

Playing on the road is never easy and particularly when you're playing a really talented team like the Bears. They beat us 21–0 and went on to win the Super Bowl.

I think that game lit the fire for us as a team in 1986.

When we went to play the Bears in Chicago it was cold. We made a decision as a group and as a team that in order to win and advance to the Super Bowl in 1986 we needed to have the playoff games at home, where we played our best ball. I think we got that attitude. We knew we had a team that could get to the Super Bowl. We just had to do it. A lot of the guys talked about it and said that the Chicago game was the game that motivated us the next year to win and go to the Super Bowl.

In 1986, we basically played the same type of defense. Pepper Johnson joined us that year and he beefed up the linebacking corps a little bit. I think we were just more competitive. We had better players and bigger players. So I think that allowed me to do more.

We ended up going 14–2 during the regular season, giving us the NFC East Championship, which was our first title since 1963.

I'd finished the 1985 season with 13 sacks and made All-Pro and the Pro Bowl like I had every year. But that wasn't my best season and I had some offseason issues prior to the 1986 season. In no way did I enter the season expecting to become the NFL's MVP. But it was gratifying to see my hard work and diligence pay off. Winning the award was far more than I could have expected.

Bill Parcells found a way to take a lot of pressure off of me, and that really helped me after coming out of rehab. At one point he warned the media: "The next guy who asks me about him is going to have trouble getting up."

Bill got ridiculed a lot that year for staying in my corner, but I think his efforts had a lot to do with me having such a good year. Because of him, I didn't have to deal with the press.

Based on what I'd been through, I know a lot of people wanted to see me fail. Athletes aren't supposed to have the same problems as people who have regular jobs. But I didn't give them the satisfaction of falling on my face. I'd always gotten motivated anytime I got told I couldn't do something. That will still piss me off. I compete with myself. So all the stuff I went through brought me motivation. And I didn't feel like I was competing just against myself, but also against all the people who wanted to see me fall flat on my face. Bill really showed that he cared for me, too. I can't tell you how many times I heard him say that he had confidence in me.

Individually, a couple of things stood out from that season.

During one six-game run I managed to get 13 sacks. Included in that run were two games against the Eagles when I had seven sacks. I also had a three-sack game against the Redskins, which wasn't an easy task given their "Hogs" up front.

Most of the time I'd line up on the right side of our defense, setting up just outside the right shoulder of Leonard Marshall, our defensive end. But I had the flexibility to roam, too.

Bill Belichick said I had a "terrific year" in 1986, and I did. Not only did I play well, but I made adjustments to the adjustments teams made against me.

Running backs blocked outside linebackers when I joined the league in 1981. I changed all of that. Nobody had done what I was doing before I got to the league, so teams had to redesign their blocking. I began to see sets with double tight ends and stuff like that. I was always at my best when I could just hunt the quarterback. That's why I lined up in different places a lot of the time.

We had a little bit of a change in our defensive philosophy that year, too. They allowed me to rush the passer more and not play the pass as much. The year before, I rushed the passer about 50 percent of the time, whereas in 1986, it was more like 80 percent of the time. That allowed me to go to the open side and do what I did best, which was run after the quarterback.

Even though 1986 was just my sixth season in the league, the NFL had already begun to take a toll on my body. I could still run, but I just wasn't as fast as I'd been and I'd get tired more easily than I once did. Some of the moves I once made I could no longer make, either. Expectations were high for me. Everybody began to expect me to do the impossible. You know, fly through the air, do a somersault, and grab the quarterback. If I wasn't doing that I wasn't being L.T. Those expectations got old. But one thing about being a veteran, I knew how to play the game well enough that I could figure out ways to compensate for all the adjustments. That's a big part of knowing how to play football. I had definitely become a smarter player by that point of my career. What made things so hard was the bullseye on my chest. Other teams looked for me by that point.

So I might have won the MVP award in 1986, but I think I had a better year in 1983.

Ray Handley Unrest

R ay Handley had the dubious distinction of following a legend. In fairness to Handley, I've got to say the man never had a chance.

Bill Parcells decided to retire after we won Super Bowl XXV. On May 15, 1991, Handley got promoted from offensive coordinator to head coach. Our defensive coordinator, Bill Belichick, had already departed to become the Browns' head coach, so George Young picked Handley.

Things did not go well from the beginning to say the least.

A big part of that wasn't his fault.

Following Parcells would have been a difficult proposition for anybody. But being the next coach to follow a legendary coach and being handed a Super Bowl–winning team on top of that ensured that he began his tenure at the top reaching for a high bar. And he got a delayed start doing so since it took the Giants so long to name him the guy.

Deciding on the starting quarterback became Handley's first big call and that, too, seemed like a no-win situation for him. Phil Simms had led the team to an 11–2 start in 1990 before suffering a season-ending injury. Our backup, Jeff Hostetler, took over and led us the rest of the way home to the Super Bowl. Either choice would be right or either choice would be wrong. So he announced an open competition between the two when most felt the job should have been

Simms' to lose. You know the old sports adage: you don't lose your job because of an injury. Actually, that adage doesn't work in the NFL. A lot of players have lost their jobs because they got injured.

At the end of training camp, Handley announced Hostetler would be the starter because he'd won the job.

We won our first game of the season against the 49ers on *Monday Night Football.* That might have been the high-water mark for a season that saw us lose three of our last four games to finish at 8–8.

The atmosphere got worse the next year when our defensive coordinator, Al Groh, left to join Belichick in Cleveland. Rod Rust became the defensive coordinator and that selection did not work out.

Rust had plenty of experience. He'd been with the Patriots when they went to Super Bowl XX in 1986 and he actually became the head coach of the Patriots in 1990, but he got fired after they went 1–15.

Nobody on the defense liked the scheme Rust wanted to play, which wasn't as aggressive as we were used to playing under Parcells.

By the middle of September of 1992, Handley had a revolt on his hands and the pot boiled over when a bunch of guys got into a shouting match with him during a game against the Cowboys. We were losing 27–0 at the half, so Handley wanted to go with the younger players in the second half because he didn't think we had a chance to win the game.

That chapped us. Carl Banks and Pepper Johnson were among the more upset.

Handley ended up letting the starters remain in the game. He also had Rust revert back to our attacking defense instead of that read-and-react shit.

Dallas scored at the start of the second half to make it 34–0 before we stormed back. In the end we lost 34–28.

Chants of "Ray must go!" became the norm at Giants Stadium. On December 30, 1992, at the end of a 6–10 season that saw us lose six of our last seven games, Handley got fired.

Handley wanted to remain in the job to fulfill the final year of his contract and told the audience for his radio show just that even though our general manager, George Young, had already told him he was finished.

Young did acknowledged the difficulty Handley faced from the beginning of his tenure due to his following Parcells. He also took part of the blame for our 14–18 record under Handley. Young surmised:

"I think it had to do with progress and team chemistry. I think the last two years were very difficult. Coming down from the mountain made it very difficult on the new coach and his staff."

The final decision came down to the fact we lacked chemistry with Ray Handley at the helm and the Giants felt it best to head in another direction with their head coach.

FINAL SEASON

Every athlete knows that the time will come when you can't play up to the level you once did any more. Time makes cowards of us all. That's one person you can't beat, Father Time.

When you lose your will to hit or be hit, it's time to get out of the game of football. I didn't want to be one of those guys who hung around too long, but I'm thankful that I had the opportunity to enjoy the game for one final season in 1993.

By the time we won our second Super Bowl, my body had pretty much seen better days.

The 1991 season marked the first season of my career I did not make the Pro Bowl after making the thing my first 10 years in the league. I only had seven sacks in 1991, and our defense just wasn't as good as it had been. I came back strong in 1992, and had been on pace for 10 sacks when I suffered a ruptured Achilles tendon in a November 8 game at Green Bay. An Achilles tear is particularly painful, so I left that game in agony riding on a golf cart. That wasn't exactly the way I wanted to go out.

That injury left me on the sidelines for the rest of the season, which turned out to be a horrible one under Ray Handley. We finished our final seven games with a 1–6 mark to go 6–10 for the season. Prior to missing those seven games, I'd only missed four games in my career due to injury. I did make a cameo appearance in the final home game of 1992 when we played the Chiefs. I limped out to midfield for the coin toss and shook hands with Chiefs quarterback Dave Krieg, then I walked off the field with my arm around O.J. Anderson.

I had mulled retirement before the 1992 season. I knew the time was close. There had been a day when all I thought about was playing football every minute of every day. Every now and then I'd think about hitting a golf shot, but mostly I just thought about football. Then the worm turned. I started to get to where I thought more about hitting those golf shots than making tackles.

Still, nobody wants to go out with an injury. Nobody wants to leave the game on somebody else's terms. I'd always joked that when the time came for me to leave football, I would march into the coach's office and say, "I want to see you." And I'd bring along my playbook instead of it being the other way around.

In my mind, I wanted at least one more season, a positive season where I could go out on my own terms. And I hoped that final season would be a winning season. By the time I played my final play, I'd always wanted fans and people in the game to remember me for contributing to the game. I wanted to be remembered as a great Giants player and one of the great players who had played any sport in New York. I wanted people to remember me to the point that when the subject of the Giants and football came up, they'd say, "Nobody played the game like Lawrence Taylor. He's the best player that's ever been."

I finally made the decision that I wanted to return for the 1993 season. So I left the golf course earlier than normal and got into the training room during the offseason at the urging of our new coach, Dan Reeves.

I didn't announce that 1993 would be my final season, but that thought had rattled around in my mind enough to where I believed it probably would be even if the season didn't turn out to be a good one. I didn't think 1993 could be any worse than 1992, when we went 6–10 under Handley.

I never regretted my decision to return for one more season. I got to smell the roses one last time, and we kicked a little ass along the way.

While Reeves made a lot of changes, he also recognized that we weren't that far removed from the Super Bowl. The genius of Reeves came in the fact he understood that we still had a bunch of guys who knew how to win, too.

With me, everybody knew I wasn't the player I'd once been. But the hope that I could rekindle the fire at different times during the game lived. And I don't think I was so far removed from greatness that I'd lost my intimidation skills. I had enough left to where offenses had to account for my whereabouts on any given play and to make sure somebody understood they had the responsibility of blocking me. Every now and then I could be counted on to rattle a quarterback as well.

I probably worked harder getting ready for the 1993 season than any other season I played. I had to in order to compete with a legend: Lawrence Taylor before the injury.

Man, I could feel it that last season, though. I'd turned 34 that year. Shit begins to hurt the older you get. And you feel the punishment you used to take and dish out so easily. During the middle of the season, I had to deal with a nagging hamstring that kept biting. I played in all 16 games, but I only started 15, and I missed a lot of action, mostly because of the hamstring. I ended up splitting time with Kanavis McGhee.

Given my physical condition and the status I'd earned with the team, I never stepped outside until Sunday during the 1993 season. I would come to practice, go to the meetings. When they went to the field, I went home. I didn't practice during the week. I'd just say, "I'll be there on Sunday." It's not a great feeling when you just don't want to be touched. If you're thinking, *Please do not hit me. Hey, I do not want to hit anybody, and do not hit me.* That's when it's time to give the game up and go on about your business.

Still, we rolled to an 11–4 record and were tied with the Cowboys, who we hosted on the final weekend of the season for the NFC East title. We were the feel-good story of the season, even if the Cowboys did beat our ass 16–13 in that game. Rodney Hampton ran for 1,077 yards, Phil Simms completed 62 percent of his passes, and we scored 83 more points than we gave up.

I finished the regular season with six sacks.

As we headed into our playoff game against the Vikings, I got asked a lot of questions about whether I planned on 1993 being my final season, or if I'd thought about our playoff game against the Vikings being my last played at Giants Stadium. I wouldn't tip my hand. All I would say was that I'd made my decision. I wasn't going to tell anybody what it was yet. I also asked the question: "If this was to be my last game at Giants Stadium, would you want me to cry going through the tunnel...or wave to all the fans? All I'm thinking about is playing the game, and if we don't focus on the game, we'll be watching the playoffs on television."

I figured that once the season was over I could look back on my career. Looking at it before the last game wasn't my style. I felt as though I didn't need to toot my own horn. I was happy with my career.

Well, we beat the Vikings 17–10 in our Wild Card game. That game was fun. We trailed 10–3 at halftime and I got a little fired up in the locker room. I stood up and told the defense we needed to shut them out the rest of the way. And we did. I even managed to get a little something going in the game, enough to prompt some "L.T.! L.T.!" cheers. When the fans were behind you, everything seemed worthwhile. You wanted to hear the chants and well-wishes, that's a part of what drives you. That day at Giants Stadium is a nice memory.

By winning, we were able to advance to play the 49ers in San Francisco the following week. That's where it ended.

San Francisco handed us our asses by a score of 44–3.

While the clock wound down I could hear the 49ers fans mocking me by yelling, "L.T.! L.T.!" like the Giants fans. The taunting didn't bother me. In a way it felt kind of like a salute. I'm thinking players that don't make a name for themselves never get taunted by the opposing fans. So instead of seething about the taunts, I'm sitting there thinking about asking referee Bernie Kukar for his penalty flag. Why not get an odd memento from my last game, right? Then I heard the final gun. I hugged Don Blackmon, our linebackers coach, then ran onto the field. The Kukar idea went away almost as quickly as it had arrived. I had an NFL security guard next to me and I asked him if he was ready to run. Then I jogged along Candlestick Park's right-field line toward our clubhouse.

In that clubhouse, I announced that I would be retiring.

When I stepped to the podium the first thing I did was hug Simms. Then I told the room, "I think it's time to pretty much call it quits." I added: "I've done everything I could do. I've been to Super Bowls. I've been to playoffs. I've been able to do things in this game that haven't been done before. I've earned the respect of players and people in general."

I understood how fortunate I'd been throughout my career and I felt damn happy that the Giants let me return for that last season. That had allowed me to play for a winning team and be a part of what felt like a resurgence to the franchise.

The final tally for my career showed 1,088 tackles with 132.5 sacks. Of course that didn't count the 9.5 sacks I had my rookie season because sacks were not an official statistic until 1982. I also had nine interceptions, two touchdowns, 33 forced fumbles, and 11 fumble recoveries.

I'd felt invincible when I arrived to the NFL in 1981, like I could do anything I wanted. A lot of people feel that way when they're young. But the time comes when you don't feel that way anymore and your body lets you know. My time had come, so I said good-bye.

No. 56 Retired

My number was retired at every level I played—high school, college, and pro. I think having the Giants retire my number was more important to me than getting into the Hall of Fame. There are a lot of Hall of Fame players who never got their number retired.

Probably one of the nicest things about the Giants retiring my number was the fact they had said they weren't going to retire any more numbers. They had planned on just putting them in the Ring of Honor instead. I didn't think that was right.

I guess Wellington Mara and George Young made a decision that they would retire one more number and that number became mine, No. 56.

I'd worn No. 89 at Lafayette High in Williamsburg, Virginia, before wearing No. 98 when I was at North Carolina. But when I got to the NFL, the league made a new rule that linebackers had to have certain numbers, and 98 wasn't one of them. That meant I had to find another number. I took No. 56, mostly because there weren't a lot of linebackers in the league wearing that number at the time and I liked that. But the possibility of my giving up that number came up that season. That brings to mind a classic story about Young.

Jim Clack had worn No. 56 in 1980. But he retired after that season, so they gave me the number. Later that season our offensive line got wiped out and that prompted our head coach, Ray Perkins, to contact Clack and convince him to return to the team. He did and finished the season as the center, but when he returned he wanted his old number back. Some of the guys, Brad Van Pelt and Brian Kelley, thought I should let Clack have his number. They told me so. That's when Young stepped in and said, "Hell no; he's going to take that number to the Hall of Fame."

It shocked the shit out of me, but I thought that was very nice of him to say that—insightful, too.

A lot of people said a lot of nice things about me prior to the night the ceremony took place. Dan Reeves, who coached the team my final season, said if I wasn't "the greatest player in franchise history," that I "certainly was one of the top ones." He noted, "The guy changed the way teams played offensive football. He made it difficult to play and plan. You had to account for him on every play."

My jersey became the eighth retired by the Giants and the first one to get retired after they honored Joe Morrison by retiring his in 1972.

The ceremony took place on October 10, 1994, at Giants Stadium during halftime of a Monday-night game against the Vikings.

I watched the first half with a bunch of family and friends from a patio next to the press box.

First, they showed video highlights of my career on the score-board, including the one that NFL Films shows a lot where I tell my teammates, "Let's go out there like a bunch of crazed dogs."

When the video show concluded, Bob Sheppard, the legendary public address announcer, said, "Ladies and gentlemen, No. 56, Lawrence Taylor."

That served as my cue to jog from a tunnel and onto a red carpet that carried me all the way to midfield. My parents were there, as were a lot of Giants executives. I remember hugging Giants co-owner Wellington Mara, who told the crowd: "Lawrence Taylor, L.T. There's nothing I can say to add to this moment. The fans have said it all. They've spoken for all of us. For 13 years, you've brought great honor to this jersey. Take care of it. No Giant will wear it again."

Wellington then presented me with a No. 56 jersey. I put on the thing and thanked him before I made my remarks.

I shared with the crowd that I wasn't nervous, because I was at home "in my house," Giants Stadium. I thanked Bill Parcells, who had been such a big part of everything in my life. Then I got to the fans.

Giants fans are the best fans in football. So I let them know that my career had been all about me and them. They'd always been there for me. I told them, "No matter what was said, no matter what was written, no matter what's been going on in my personal life, we've always been in this together. Without you guys, there would've been a Lawrence Taylor, but there wouldn't have been an L.T."

Once I said that, they gave me a standing ovation and began with the chant of "L.T.! L.T.!" I loved that. How could I not?

Afterward, I hopped in a golf cart and took a lap around the field. I can't tell you how great I felt seeing so many fans wearing No. 56 jerseys. And there were the banners. Just for that night they lifted the ban on banners at Giants Stadium.

The moment proved to be one of the three most memorable I had at Giants Stadium, including the 13–10 overtime win over Dallas in 1981 that earned us our first playoff berth since 1963, and the 17–0 win over the Redskins in 1987 that earned us a trip to our first Super Bowl. Yes, that was quite a special night that I was able to enjoy with the people I'm close to and all the special Giants fans.

Clutch Catch:
Phil Simms to L.T.

I played a lot of football in my life. During my career I managed to play some pretty good football in some big games, too. So it's funny that the night of September 4, 1995, I felt more nervous than I'd ever felt on a football field during the halftime ceremony of a Cowboys–Giants game at Giants Stadium.

Phil Simms got his jersey retired that night and he decided to call me into action as a receiver.

Phil didn't invite me that night. You have to understand, we'd had an argument a couple of years before, and we hadn't talked up until that point. Still, I went to that game. I knew they were going to honor Phil. I thought I should be there and give my congratulations. So I was standing in the tunnel when Phil came by. He saw me and came over to me. We embraced and it was kind of like, *Damn, why haven't we talked in three years?* So we started talking and he said, "I want you to come out on the field with me. Will you come out on the field with me?" I said I would.

The ceremony turned out to be a first-class affair with strobe lights, his family present, and all kinds of fancy stuff.

Phil looked immaculate, dressed to the nines in a white shirt and tie while Wellington Mara handled the introductions. Giants Stadium swelled with fans wanting to see Phil recognized and to see him once again wear his No. 11 jersey. Once he put on that jersey, the crowd of 77,454 offered a booming standing ovation.

Phil thanked everybody that night, George Young in particular. He had been the guy who had the balls to select a quarterback from Morehead State with the Giants' No. 1 pick in 1979.

Phil made a great speech. He talked with emotion about loving the game and having a passion for the game, but knowing one day it would end. He concluded by noting that he asked just two things of the Giants that night. He wanted to run out on the field and wear No. 11 and he wanted to throw a final pass. That's where I came in.

I hadn't done anything athletic in I don't know how long and there was Phil telling this packed house of Giants fans that he wants to throw his last pass to one of the greatest Giants players of all time, Lawrence Taylor. So I was standing about 10 yards away and I said, "Throw it here."

Phil wouldn't have that. He told me, "Go." I was like, "What the hell are you talking about, 'Go?'" And I'd been drinking a little bit, too. So I took off and he was like, "Keep going, keep going." All of a sudden he just heaved one. I sped up trying to get to the ball, and all I could think about is, *You can't drop this pass. You've got to catch up to it.* Then, *If you drop this pass, you may as well move to the moon.*

When that ball finally landed in my arms I felt relieved. I cradled that thing, then ran back to Phil so I could hand him the ball and give him a bear hug.

It's funny; I was more nervous on that play than I was at any time during my playing career.

WELLINGTON MARA

What I'll always remember about Wellington Mara was the fact that even though he was the owner, he seemed like a player. After every game, the first person you'd see come into the locker room was Wellington. If we won, he had this broad smile on his face and he'd congratulate everyone. When we lost, he'd tell everybody to keep their head up. He was one of us. He attended all the games and almost every practice.

I will always be grateful for how well he treated me. When I got into trouble, he stood by me. I never believed he did so because I was Lawrence Taylor, either. I felt like he would have done that for anybody in the Giants family. In my opinion, Mr. Mara was the greatest thing that ever happened to the Giants. He'd always be there to help even when I wasn't making the best decisions and wasn't exactly willing to help myself. He'd tell me if I was doing something wrong, but he didn't reprimand me. I considered him a friend.

He didn't say a lot, but what he said would stick.

Despite his wealth, he was a man of simple tastes. The story about his wife Ann giving him a pair of expensive Italian leather loafers spoke volumes. He would not wear those shoes despite his wife's desire for him to do so. He finally gave in, but he cut off the gold buckles on the top. He felt like they made the shoes look too fancy.

The Giants joined the NFL in 1925 and have been one of the

strongest franchises in the league, thanks largely to the Mara family. Timothy J. Mara originally purchased the team for $500 before he turned the team over to his sons, Wellington and Jack.

Jack died in 1965 and Wellington, the younger of the two sons, took over. Think about that transition. He'd actually been a ball boy when the team played its first game. That's how he got the nickname "Duke." The players found out he'd been named Wellington after the Duke of Wellington. By 1941, the Wilson football used in NFL games became "The Duke" in honor of Wellington Mara.

Wellington concentrated on football decisions for the Giants during the first 37 years of his tenure with the team. He turned over some of his daily duties to Andy Robustelli in 1974 in advance of making one of his wisest decisions with the Giants by hiring George Young as the team's first general manager after the 1978 season.

Wellington and Tim J. Mara, his nephew who inherited his brother's stake in the team, didn't get along. They didn't even speak, which made things difficult for the operation of the team.

A lot of people attributed the "Miracle at the Meadowlands"—a November 1978 game that saw the Giants turn a sure victory into a defeat on the final play—as a contributing factor for giving the Wellington and Tim a wake-up call that a change needed to be made. That facilitated the hiring of Young, to whom they gave full control of football operations.

Three years later, the Giants made the playoffs for the first time since 1963.

Other than a three-year stint in the Navy during World War II, he remained involved in the operation of the Giants for nearly 80 years.

Perhaps one of the most lasting parts of his legacy is the fact that he embraced splitting the millions of dollars in television revenues he could have made being in New York with the other owners. He saw the wisdom of the nation's largest market splitting revenues with the small-market teams of the league. He saw them as partners. That's one of the big reasons the NFL is the most successful of all the professional sports leagues today.

He was enshrined in the Pro Football Hall of Fame in 1997.

Mr. Mara remained a co-owner of the team until he died in 2005. Upon his death, then-commissioner Paul Tagliabue said:

> *Wellington Mara represented the heart and soul of the National Football League. He was a man of deep conviction who stood as a beacon of integrity. When Well Mara stood to speak at a league meeting, the room would become silent with anticipation because all of us knew we were going to hear profound insights born of eight decades of league experience.*

He was so beloved that the other NFL owners postponed three days of meetings once the news of his death broke.

Fittingly, in the first game following his death, the Giants beat the Redskins—the Giants' biggest rivals according to Wellington—36–0 at Giants Stadium. The 78,630 fans in attendance at Giants Stadium that day gave him a standing ovation when his name was mentioned.

Wellington Mara was one of the best people around. There aren't a lot of people who are all about others. He never thought about himself. He wanted the best for the fans, the players, and the team. Thank goodness for me he was a religious man and went to Mass every day. He believed in second chances. He always was one of the best men I'd ever been around.

HALL OF FAME

My induction ceremony for the Pro Football Hall of Fame took place on August 7, 1999, in Canton, Ohio.

Joining me on the podium that day were fellow inductees Eric Dickerson, the NFL's third leading career rusher; Tom Mack, a guard who played 13 years for the Los Angeles Rams; Ozzie Newsome, a tight end for the Cleveland Browns; and Billy Shaw, a guard for the Buffalo Bills from 1961 to '69 who became the first Hall of Fame Player to spend his entire career in the old American Football League.

I became the last of the five to get inducted, making me inductee No. 199, which earned me the distinction of being the final inductee of the millennium.

My parents were there, as were my ex-wife and three of my children.

My oldest son, T.J., introduced me, and he really did a nice job. I was touched. But I think the biggest thing that happened during that ceremony was that Harry Carson showed up.

We'd had a rift. I had thought Harry was a hater because every time he turned around it seemed like he was always saying something negative about me or something like that. So we had stopped talking. I hadn't talked to Harry in about three or four years at that time. So I went to the Hall of Fame ceremony and even though we weren't talking, he found his way. Harry came to the ceremony. I saw

180

him and I mentioned him during my speech.

When the ceremony was over, and I was in the back room with Harry and his wife, he hugged me and offered me congratulations. I thought that showed so much class, man. I started crying. I couldn't believe that he came to the Hall of Fame to be with me on my most important day. And we have been the best of friends, again, ever since.

So here's how it went that day, from my son's speech as my presenter to my speech as the inductee:

Lawrence Taylor Jr. (presenter):

I would like to begin by saying today is a wonderful day. Today is the day we put my father, who I think is the greatest linebacker of all time, in a place where he belongs, the Pro Football Hall of Fame. A man who was such a dominant force, he changed the way the game was played. Today is the day we put my father into the place where legends live, the Pro Football Hall of Fame.

It is with great pride and pleasure that I am able to stand before you today to present such a great person, friend, and father. When I was young growing up in New Jersey, where I live now, I knew my dad was special. But not only to me, but to other people. When I was young, going to school, people used to ask me to get my dad to sign all kinds of things. And I was even more convinced then that my dad was special, not only to me but to them, too. When I reached my teens and read about all his accomplishments on the field and his mishaps off the field, that helped me know, love, and respect my father even more. Those stories made me understand why people admired him so much. Sure, I admired him, too—not because of L.T. the football player; 'cause of Lawrence Taylor, my father. I admire my father because he is never one to not admit he made a mistake. I love my father. I would do anything for him, just as well as he would do anything for me or my other sisters, Whitney, Tanisha, and Paula. If I could pick anybody to be my father, I would pick Lawrence Taylor every time. Me and my father have a good relationship. We talk all the time, one-on-one, we go to the movies, go bowling; just spending time together with him is very special to me. And it's very special to him too. He is not only a friend to me, he's a friend to my friends as well, because he knows how special friends are. Doc, Pritchard, Stone, Cosmo, J.D. and my god-father Paul Davis, or as he would say, "the Fellas," are his old friends from high school which he is still close to, which he loves and I love, too. My father wants the best for me just as well as his parents wanted the best for him growing up in Williamsburg, Virginia. Most of all I would like to say thank you to my father for being there for me, and never letting me settle for less. And even though he might not admit it, I thank Ron Jaworski for making my father what he [became], 'cause without him he probably would have never broken that sack record. And on behalf of my father, I will thank you fans of New York, fans here of Cleveland for lighting the fire that was in my father when he played. And like he says, "Without you, there would have been a Lawrence Taylor, but there would not have been an L.T., and I thank you for that." So before I bring my father up here, can I hear that L.T. chant?

Lawrence Taylor:
You know Bill Parcells…I had a bet with Bill Parcells that I wouldn't cry; well, he almost won the bet right there because I almost lost it. But I got my composure. You know, when I first came out here today…thank you…I guess we was walking, the program was just about to begin, and I was a little bit nervous, and God I was, what I was going to say, and the excitement was running through my head, and I really was a little nervous. Then I came out, and I looked through the

glass and I saw all the Giant uniforms, all the Giants stuff, and I knew right then and there I was in L.T. territory, and I love it. Thank you.

You know it's a pleasure and an honor, and I do understand what it means to be in the Football Hall of Fame. Going up a lot of great guys. There's a lot of guys gone before me and I sit back and I try to think of how did I get here. Not just through football, not just through my play, because, you know, that's God-given talent. That's working with a lot of great teammates, great individuals. But I look around and I figure out who I have to thank for the opportunities and the position I am in right now, and I thank so many people. First of all I want to thank the Giant fans, guys, I tell you what. You know we all have great abilities, we all can play ball, we all can run, we can tackle, we can hit, we can run, we can jump, but if you have no one you can do that for then it's not worth a thing, you know. So I'm glad I had to do it for you guys, and I'm glad I had the opportunity.

I have a lot of friends here today. Giants fan friends, my personal friends. I have "the Fellas" from Williamsburg, Virginia, where I grew up. And hey, what's happening, boys. And I have my friends from my hometown. I have from New Jersey, Gary Gagliotta, Deano, Eric. Vicky, Vicky right now, she is the most important thing right now to me simply 'cause she gets everything done for me. My life is very chaotic as you can tell, and without her working every day, trying to get me together, I couldn't do it. I'd like to thank you, thank you very much.

I have cousins, cousins, and cousins, and cousins, and cousins, and cousins, and cousins. I'd also like to thank my teammates. Some of my teammates came out today. You know, O.J. Anderson, Gary Jeter, George Martin. And guys, let me tell you about this other teammate out here today.

You know, me and this guy, we had some words a while back and we kind of split ways and we just didn't really talk, but I tell you, Harry Carson came out for me today, and that's the classiest thing I've ever seen in my life, Harry. Thank you, thank you. I love you, man. I love you. Laura and her dad. His wife. And my best friend in the whole world, Paul Davidson and his wife. He's been with me for a lot of years. A lot of years. A lot of years.

Now I go to my family. I'd like to thank my family for being here, and being with me. My mom and my dad, right here. Why don't you stand, stand. My brother, my two brothers. Clarence, Kim, and his wife and kids. Wife and kids. My loving ex-wife, loving ex-wife. Seriously, Linda Taylor…stand up, girl. And her mother, my in-laws, ex-in-laws. Even though they're my ex, I still love them all, I love them all, I love everyone. But you know, I'd like to thank so many people. I'd like to thank Linda for putting up with me for so many years. I'd like to thank my parents for really just working with me. And when I was a young boy, I said I was going to do certain things and they always believed in me to do the right thing. And I'm very appreciative that I had the opportunity to do for them also. And I'd like to thank my kids. I tell you what, I'd like to thank my kids for understanding people do make mistakes in life. And somehow they have the ability to forgive me and love me anyway. And I thank you for that.

There's a host of people here that I know I am just forgetting people, and all that. But, I would like to talk about, you know, as far as my football career, you know, there's been like three people in my football career that's been really, really instrumental and the most important things to me as far as football goes through my football career. There's three men, and one of those men happens to be George Young. George Young, our general manager from the New York Giants. Let me tell you, this guy, he drafted me. A lot of people asked him why, until they saw the tapes. Anyway, but George has always been in my corner. He's always helped me push to do better, to stay out of trouble, whatever. And do the right thing. And George has always been there for me and I'd like to thank him, right there. Thank you, George.

There's another man that's very important, and he's been instrumental. You know, you talk about the George Halases, you talk about the Paul Browns, you talk about all the great owners in the league. Let me tell you something, you're doing yourself an injustice if you don't talk about Wellington Mara. Wellington Mara. It's truly been a pleasure. And let me tell you, all you Giants fans, you know, Wellington Mara is a person who really loves his football team. This guy has stood behind me for a lot of years, on the field and off the field. Without him I probably would not be here today. So I want to thank Wellington Mara for his kindness and generosity. Thank you, Wellington.

And I'd like to thank a coach, that without him...man, I tell you, he's the coach of coaches, in my opinion. Bill Parcells, I have never in my life had a coach that knew the game of football as well and knew me as well and was able to put the two together and make a great combination. This guy is instrumental, and I was asked about Bill—do we talk anymore? Well, it's like a marriage that's lasted 30 years. You really don't talk that much but you know you love each other anyway. And that's the way Bill and [I are] now. I wish he could be here, but he has situations in New York and I understand and I love him dearly. Without Bill Parcells, I tell you, I would not been able to do the things I was able to do.

And lastly guys, thank you, and lastly, you know people ask me all the time, well the Hall of Fame, you're in the Hall of Fame. What do you want to leave to other people? What do you want other people to remember? What kind of legacy do you want to leave behind? And I thought about that. And it's indeed a great honor to be here. But the thing I want to leave all the people is that, you guys, life, like anything else, can knock you down. It can turn you out. You'll have problems everyday in your life. But sometimes, like Ozzie Newsome said, sometimes you just got to go play. You just got to go play. And no matter how many times it knocks you down. No matter how many times you think you can't go forward. No matter how many times things just don't go right. You know, anybody can quit. Anybody can do that. A Hall of Famer never quits. A Hall of Famer realizes that, a Hall of Famer realizes that the crime is not being knocked down, the crime is not getting up again. And I want to thank you for allowing me to be here. Thank you very much.

JOE MONTANA: THE BEST

Because chasing quarterbacks became my calling card during my career, I'm asked a lot about who I think is the best quarterback.

A lot of people like Peyton Manning, particularly after he won his second Super Bowl, or Tom Brady, who has won four. Some would go with John Elway or Dan Marino. I just don't see any of them being better than Joe Montana. He's the best I've played against and the best I've seen. Why? First, I'll say this: I'm old-school and that casts a vote for Montana right off the bat.

We did some good things against the 49ers when Joe played quarterback for them. We beat them in the playoffs following the 1985 and 1986 seasons. And we beat them on our way to Super Bowl XXV, too. Still, Joe did plenty of damage against us. I played against him enough to know what he could do. He pretty much had it all and he did it during an era when the rules didn't favor the quarterback like they do now.

Today's game is almost like touch football out there the way the defense can't hit anybody, particularly the quarterback. The way it is now reminds me of those 7-on-7 games that the kids play in the summer. Those are like drills. A quarterback who can see the field and throw the football to the right guy with anything on the ball is going to do well.

We put a lot of licks on Montana. He always came back unless he physically couldn't. He was tough. You always had to respect what he might do to you on the next play. If we hadn't been around to beat the 49ers in some big games, he might have played in eight Super Bowls. He also led Kansas City to an AFC championship game against Buffalo.

Of course, Montana is my era, so I sound a little bit like the old guy who always says football was a lot tougher of a game when he played.

Montana played in four Super Bowls and the 49ers won each of them. He also won three Super Bowl MVP Awards and threw 11 touchdowns with no interceptions. That's pretty close to perfection.

A lot of people might point to Joe having four Super Bowl rings as the reason why I think he's the best, but that's not the case. Take the rings out of the picture. I mean, Terry Bradshaw had four, too. And, of course, Brady's been to six and won four rings. Still, to me it's all about how a quarterback commands a game. Joe commanded a game like nobody I've ever seen. That's where I'd give Joe the advantage over John Elway and Dan Marino—the two guys a lot of people label as the best-ever quarterbacks. Both of those guys had great arms, they just didn't command a game like Joe did.

The teams Joe guided beat teams guided by Elway and Marino in the Super Bowl by a combined score of 93–26 in two games.

All I can go by for Brady and Manning is what I've seen on TV. I haven't seen either command a game like Joe did. Of course, I haven't seen the same thing from any other quarterbacks, either.

If the offense had its way, Joe could lay the points on a defense like he did in his five-touchdown performance against Denver in the Super Bowl. If he faced a really formidable defense, he could usually find a way to win. Take his signature game-winning drive against the Bengals in Super Bowl XXIII, when he took the 49ers the length of the field before throwing a 10-yard touchdown to John Taylor to seal the deal.

In fairness to Manning, I didn't play against him. That means I can't sense what he's like as a competitor from watching on TV like I could with Joe.

I do think Joe had a great cast of players around him. And I definitely think he had the good fortune to play in Bill Walsh's system. Those two came together perfectly and at just the right time to run that offense.

Simply stated, Joe Montana was a great competitor and the No. 1 quarterback of all time in my estimation.

Speaking of the J-E-T-S

Questions about the Giants–Jets rivalry come naturally, since the teams share a huge sports market. The thing is, I just never considered the Jets much of a rival. The way I looked at it as a player and the way I look at it now is the same: the Giants own New York.

The Jets are the ugly stepsister in New York. They were the other team and always will be the other team. You just never talked about them. They're one of those teams that has it all, but never does anything with it. We were pretty much the top dogs when I played for the Giants. Our record and everything spoke for itself. That's the way it was then, and that's the way it still seems to be.

The Giants have been around since 1925. The Jets started out as the Titans in the old American Football League. They had some early moments when Joe Namath played quarterback back in the 1960s, but they haven't done anything since Namath led them to that big upset over the Baltimore Colts in the third Super Bowl. That was 1969. We've won four Super Bowls since then and been to five. On top of that, we've been to the playoffs 15 times. Yes, the Jets have played in the postseason 13 times since Broadway Joe gave the Jets their greatest moment. They've just never been back to the Super Bowl.

You know what, I thought the Jets had some good teams during the era when they had the "Sack Exchange"—Mark Gastineau, Joe Klecko, Marty Lyons, and Abdul Salaam—that played really well for a year or so. They had some decent players. I don't think they've had anything special at quarterback since dadgum Namath, though. They've had a couple of good ones, but nobody really jumped out at you.

I've always said that Jets fans were Giants fans who couldn't get tickets to Giants games. We've got a lot more fans than the Jets and our fans are better fans, too. Even our uniforms are better. Classic blue compared to the Jets' green. The way I see it, unless they start winning some Super Bowls, pretty soon, there's no conversation about this subject.

Now, I'm not saying the Jets have bad fans. The New York area is a great place to play because the fans know sports and they are passionate about their sports and the teams they follow. I will say this: we knew we wanted to beat the Jets when we played them. You wanted to have bragging rights, particularly since we shared the same stadium, though we were the main tenants.

Today the Giants and Jets share MetLife Stadium, which seats 82,500 fans and has a lot of bells and whistles.

Obviously, the teams don't play every year because they aren't in the same division. Maybe if they did, the rivalry would be better. And don't talk about the yearly exhibition game. Man, that game means less than nothing.

Even the first one I played in didn't seem to matter much.

The Jets had won five in a row against the Giants when we met them on a Saturday night at Giants Stadium in August of 1981. Included in that run had been the previous year's 32–7 romp by the Jets when Richard Todd threw four touchdown passes.

We were a 2–0 team at that point of the exhibition season, but keeping our undefeated record intact for games that don't count just didn't matter.

So their 37–24 win hardly upset the apple cart where we were concerned. I did see a little more excitement from the fans for that one than I did for the other exhibition games. Still, it just didn't matter. We pulled to within three points at 20–17 after Johnny Perkins caught a 24-yard touchdown late in the third quarter. Then our regulars pretty much left the game. That validated the message that the winner of that game didn't matter.

We did have some pretty good games during my playing days.

My rookie season we played them on November 1, 1981, and they beat us 26–7. The "Sack Exchange" was in full stride that season. They went on to do us a huge favor that year by beating the Packers on the final day of the season. They played the Packers at home and came away with a 28–3 win. The Jets' win combined with our 13–10 overtime win over Dallas put us into the playoffs with a 9–7 record. They went into the playoffs with a 10–5–1 record. And they felt pretty good about themselves.

After our coach, Ray Perkins, toasted the Jets for beating Green Bay, Jets quarterback Richard Todd noted, "I think the Giants should really appreciate us. Well, they backed up into it. They didn't give us anything. We gave it to them."

Todd might have been cocky, but he was right. The Jets helped us out big time that season.

We didn't play the Jets again until 1984, and we won 20–10 that day. The Jets only gained 67 yards on the ground in that game, but Ken O'Brien threw for 351 yards.

In 1987, we both finished 6–9, but we beat them 20–7 in the last game of the season.

Mark Bavaro had a monster game that day, catching six passes for 109 yards and a touchdown. That finished off that horrific strike season on a high note.

They came back and beat us 27–21 in 1988 when Al Toon caught a five-yard touchdown from O'Brien with 37 seconds to play. That loss pissed me off, because it came on the last weekend of the season and kept us out of the playoffs.

I'll tell you what; if the Giants and the Jets ever met in the Super Bowl, now that would be something. But I'll believe it when I see it.

TODAY'S NFL

The game is more popular than it's ever been, if you believe the ratings. People love their teams, and everybody seems to do that fantasy football shit.

I don't really watch a lot of the NFL these days. I'm just not the guy who's going to sit home with my eyes glued to the TV. If I'm sitting home, believe me, football is not on the TV. Now, if I'm at a bar, I may watch it. If the Giants are on in a sports bar, I'll watch it. I'm always interested in what the Giants do, as well as some of the other teams around the league. The league has just changed so much since I played. I think it's a safer game now. But they couldn't pay me enough to play now.

Today it seems like they're throwing the ball on every play. At least two-thirds of the time, the ball's in the air. I remember back when I was playing you had 31 passes and 33 runs. The play calling was more balanced. Now you have 50, 60 passes a game, and the ball is in the air a lot. I don't like the way it is. I don't know exactly when it changed, but it's affected other things within the game—like wide receivers.

Back in my day, wide receivers didn't talk shit. Because once they'd come across that middle, we could hit them. We could lay them out. Wide receivers were pretty humble back when I played.

Nowadays, they're the ones who've got all the mouth. They're the ones talking all the shit because they can run all over the place. The game of football wasn't meant to be played where the wide receivers have so much to say like they do now.

Don't get me wrong. Wide receivers are great athletes. You just can't hit them. You can't reroute them. It's like a field day. They can go wherever the hell they want. Shit, I would be a wide receiver now.

Tackling is a different animal these days, too.

When I learned to play football, we were taught from grade school on to drive your helmet into the gut of the guy with the ball and ride it up underneath his chin. I liked to use the whole body. But I wasn't trying to tackle like that because I wanted to be a weapon. Back then we called that form tackling—face mask into the chest and rip up. That would stop a lot of people. And when you used to see somebody slide their head to the right or slide their head to the left, you used to call them chicken, man. "You scared to hit somebody? What's wrong with you? What the hell are you ducking your head for?"

But that's not the way you tackle now. If you do it the old-fashioned way, you'll get a 15-yard penalty at the very least. You'll probably end up getting suspended a game or two, too. If the mentality I had as a player was going on in today's game, I'd be fined, suspended, and banging heads with the league all the time. Things have changed so much. They will fine you for just about anything now. Playing in the NFL is more of a job these days than a game. An NFL game isn't about a bunch of boys out there flying around and having fun anymore; it's like a corporate thing now.

Whether the change has been good or bad is not for me to say. I'm quite sure the change has saved some concussions and stuff. But if you can't tackle somebody hard, let them feel you, you lose some of your intimidation, too. How do you instill fear into a player if you can't make contact—serious contact—with them? That's how you make guys afraid of you. I always prided myself on being a clean player. But when I went through you, I went through you. The NFL has changed so much and I'm not sure it's been for the best.

CHAPTER 4

OFF THE FIELD

LOVE OF GOLF

I never played golf growing up, but I got interested in the sport once I got to the NFL. I've loved golf ever since.

Once I got to the Giants, my agent at the time got me interested in trying out golf.

Like a lot of athletes, I had a lot of free time on my hands, so he thought I might like golf and I just started playing. I'm glad I did.

With the Giants it seemed like we always were involved in some kind of tournament during the offseason. Learning to play the game probably saved me a lot of embarrassment.

Most don't think a burly guy like me can swing a golf club. You always hear all the same things about football players being too bulky to hit the ball the right way. That's a bunch of B.S., though I have seen plenty of bad golfers who happened to be football players.

Football fans always knew me for my quickness, but most figured I was some kind of brute on the golf course. Or that the golf course wasn't the place for a football player because they're all musclebound and lose their temper. Not true. If I'm out on the golf course and have a 160-yard shot to a green, I'll take out a 9 iron and smooth one. You don't have to come out of your shoes. Golf has always been a relaxing game for me. Hitting that little white ball is not a lot like football. It requires some finesse.

One of the reasons I like the sport is it allows you to disappear into the game. When I'm out on the golf course, I'm never thinking about my day-to-day worries while I'm planning a shot or figuring out what club to hit. Being out there on the course seems to refresh me for all the other things I have to tackle.

I've been fortunate to meet a lot of people while playing golf. You can get to know a lot about a person while spending four hours out on the course with them. I love all the different courses. All of them seem to have their own personality the way they're built. But I think I mostly just like the game itself. There are so many challenges to the sport and you can never totally conquer the game.

I rarely participated in the Giants' offseason conditioning program. Being out on the golf course worked better for me. There's two ways of looking at it. Most players looked at the offseason like the time they needed to get in great shape for the season, get all jacked up to handle the punishment. To me, I stayed in shape, but I didn't want to arrive to camp mentally spent. If I was ready mentally for the season, that allowed everything else to fall into place for me. I always got a lot of work in at camp, too.

Right now I'm a 3 handicap. I've been lower. I don't practice like I used to, though. I used to really enjoy practicing. Now I play more than I practice. I might hit a few balls, but I figure, why bother? My swing ain't going to change too much. Putting is the best part of my game. I can't tell you how many times I've heard, "You've got a wonderful touch for a big man."

You're not going to see me playing 54 holes of golf in a day much anymore. That's a good day. I used to do that a lot, but that was a long time ago. I'm an 18-hole man.

Relative to a lot of my peers, I left football fairly healthy. I'm not handicapped or anything like that. I got out of the game pretty intact. That's allowed me to continue enjoying golf without the pain that might have prevented me from doing that. I quit playing golf for a while during my drug years. But when I came out of rehab in '99, I picked up the golf clubs again, and I've been playing every day since.

What do I like about the game? Well, there are a lot of things.

For starters, it's a game you can never totally beat. You can play it well, but there's always something you could have done better in any round you play. Next, you have the great layouts. Every golf course is different. You're out there on this beautiful piece of property with close-cropped grass and you're competing against yourself. Once I took up the game I instantly appreciated the solitude.

People knew who I was once I joined the Giants. Obviously New York is the biggest market anywhere. That made me more recognizable than most and that translated to celebrity. I like that people know who I am, but getting asked to sign an autograph everywhere I go can get old. The golf course gave me a place where I could go and people wouldn't bother me.

Golfers are always working on something. Maybe their chipping is bad or they've got this incurable slice. So they're worried about their own game. They're not like, "That's Lawrence Taylor; let's go get an autograph." I'll still get that some on the golf course, but it's not like I get it on the street. On the golf course you can just relax, you know.

I don't really have any golf stories, but here's one about me that Phil Mickelson shared from the 1994 Bob Hope Chrysler Classic. It appeared in the April 2005 edition of *Golf Digest*:

> *I played in the celebrity rotation with Joe Pesci, Mike Ditka, and Lawrence Taylor. When we got to the 18th hole, Ditka hit a couple of shots in the water. Then Pesci hit a couple of shots in the water. And then Lawrence Taylor hit a couple of shots in the water. So my ball was the only one that counted when we got up to the green.*

> *Well, my birdie putt looked good from the moment I stroked it. When it got about 18 inches from the hole, I started walking because I could tell the ball was going right in the middle of the cup.*

Then all of a sudden, out of nowhere, another ball came rolling onto the green, hit my ball in mid-roll and deflected it off its path. I looked over in the direction where the ball came from, and Lawrence Taylor was standing there with this sheepish look on his face. He had been practice-putting and hit my ball.

"Sorry," he said.

Well, I was really hacked off and started walking toward him to give him a piece of my mind. But he got bigger and bigger as I got closer and closer—and all I could get out of my mouth was: "No problem, L.T."

I've been very fortunate. I've played with a lot of different people. I've played a lot of different courses. And I can tell you I just have a fun time playing. I think any day I'm on the golf course is a good one. I mean, I'll play in rain, I'll play in snow. I don't care. If I want to get out there I'm going to get out there and play.

Playing golf brings me some of the most fun I've had off the football field.

DANCING WITH THE STARS

Competing on *Dancing with the Stars* brought a lot of fun my way. I'll tell you the truth, though. That's something I would never do again. It's a lot of work. It's a lot more work than you think.

When I got the opportunity to be on the show in 2009, I looked at the thing as a chance to get myself back into shape. I'd always had some kind of exercise regimen, and I'd kind of gotten away from that at that point in my life. Dancing is major exercise. You're moving your body in all different directions.

I knew other football players such as Jerry Rice, Emmitt Smith, Warren Sapp, and Jason Taylor had all appeared on the show. Smith won and Rice came in second. It was so funny. I saw Taylor on the show and I watched a little bit of it. I came away thinking, "Shit, I know dadgum well that I'm a better dancer than Jason Taylor." But hey, every dance we had to do, I'd never heard of—the Paso Doble Dance, the Cha-Cha. Man, I'd never heard of any of this shit. It was rough, I'll tell you, especially when you get to a point where you don't really want to be there anymore.

Aside from wanting to get myself back into shape, the competitive aspect of the thing interested me as well. I went into it planning to win; make no mistake about it. I'm a competitor and a fighter. I wanted to do my best and I didn't want to embarrass myself or my family.

I knew going in that there were much better dancers on the show. But I figured nobody would work harder than me. I quickly learned that practicing dancing was a lot different than practicing for football. I was 50 years old back then.

Professional dancer Edyta Swilinska became my partner. Working with her helped to no end. She was a blessing, man. She knew how to get the best out of me. Nobody worked harder than she did.

Preparing for the show, we practiced at least 20 hours a week. Those were incredible workouts and they were different than anything I'd done in the past. I dropped about 25 pounds, because you have to work every day. For example, even if I had to be in New York, my partner had to go with me. Wherever I went, she had to go with me. She had to fly with me. Your partner has to go with you because you have to work every day. You're talking about six hours a day. The group of celebrities we competed against included actress Denise Richards, rapper Lil' Kim, Apple cofounder Steve Wozniak, Go-Go's singer Belinda Carlisle, comedian David Alan Grier, Olympic gymnast Shawn Johnson, actor Gilles Marini, *Jackass* star Steve-O, and songwriter Chuck Wicks.

The dances I practiced and learned were really technical, like the ballroom dancing. I learned all the technical stuff the judges would look for, like how to point my toe and a lot of other stuff.

You get lulled into a false sense of security, because you have a month to work on two dances. Everybody is there for the first month—the first two shows of the season. You don't get cut until the second show. So you have to do two dances. And you have a month to learn them.

But, after that, if you stay on the show, you have to learn a dance in four days. Then as you go longer in the thing, you have to learn two dances in four days. It's just too much work. I'll tell you; you're trying to do things here, you're trying to do things there. What a mess.

I mean, I wanted to go home. I probably hadn't seen a golf club in two months. It got rough for me. After eight weeks I didn't want any more. I mean, shit, I wanted to go home.

Ultimately, we were eliminated during the seventh week of competition after we scored a 21 out of 30 possible points for our waltz. That was the lowest score of the week. We got the axe based on a combination of the judges' scores from that night and the home viewers' votes. They cast votes immediately following the broadcast.

Here's what some of the judges said of our performance.

Bruno Tonioli: "When you're turning you get a little bit clumsy. And then there was a little incident at the reveal where you lost balance, which is a shame. It's not terrible, but not brilliant."

Carrie Ann Inaba: "Here's what I saw; I actually saw more freedom in your movement. I don't know what's going on, but you're movement is a little more open, you look like you're really enjoying it."

And Len Goodman directed this comment my way: "You captured the grace of the dance; it has a tenderness about it and an elegance. Overall, I was shocked about how well you performed it."

Dancing with the Stars host Tom Bergeron caught me smiling after we got eliminated. I cracked up when he said, "Can I just tell you— you're the worst actor we've ever had on this show. You're the happiest guy to get home [and] to get back to the golf course."

And he was right. I was happy to get eliminated.

After we were out, six couples remained, and out of those there were some really phenomenal dancers. We might not have won, but in our rearview mirror we had taken care of business against Belinda Carlisle, Denise Richards, Holly Madison, Steve Wozniak, David Alan Grier, and Steve-O.

Shawn Johnson and her partner, Mark Ballas, ended up winning.

Overall, *Dancing with the Stars* was an amazing experience. Along the way I did learn how to dance pretty well. I don't know where the hell I'm going to use it, but I know how to do it.

ACTING CAREER

A cting is a pursuit I've enjoyed since my playing days ended.
Here's a list of some of the things I've done before a camera:
One episode of *Married...with Children*, one episode of *Coach*,
multiple episodes of *1st & Ten*, *The Waterboy*, *Any Given Sunday*,
Shaft, *Mercy Streets*, one episode of *Body & Soul*, one episode of *The
Sopranos*, one episode of *Las Vegas*, and *In Hell*.

I've also been a voice for the video games *Grand Theft Auto: Vice
City* and *Blitz: the League 2*.

Of all of the movies and shows I've been a part of, I probably
enjoyed working on *In Hell* and *Any Given Sunday* the most.

Ringo Lam directed *In Hell*, and Jean-Claude Van Damme was
the star of the show. He played Kyle LeBlanc, a man who decides to
take the law into his own hands to avenge his murdered wife. That
lands him in prison with a life sentence. We end up in a cell together.
I'm simply Inmate 451, a badass with a reputation for killing. By the
end of the movie, I help him escape and all that shit.

My most visible role came in director Oliver Stone's *Any Given
Sunday*. I play Luther "Shark" Lavay, an aging star linebacker who
knows his way around the league. Sound familiar?

That role proved to be a lucky one for me.

Playing Shark allowed me to have some pretty big scenes, like
when he throws a wild party at his house or when he begs for an

injection so he can play on game day. My most acclaimed scene from the movie comes in the steam room, when Shark lends advice to the team's cocky quarterback, Willie Beamen.

A lot of people have asked me how much of that role was acting and how much of the role was just playing Lawrence Taylor. I tell them I really don't know.

It's funny how I got that part. I read for it when I was in rehab. And Oliver Stone wanted me to read for the part. I went to New York to do so, and I didn't do very well. But he said he would consider me.

But then I went to rehab—and actually, I was only supposed to stay in rehab for 30 days. But I ended up having to stay for 65 days. So by the time they were ready to shoot the movie, I was still in rehab.

When I got out Oliver asked me to come down to Florida to be a technical advisor or some shit like that. So I did. I remember going to the set where they were practicing football. At that time they had Michael Clarke Duncan playing the part of Shark.

They ran a couple of plays, and then they had a play where Duncan had to hit a guy. After watching the play, Oliver looked at me and he said, "I just don't feel it. I just don't feel it."

A couple of minutes later, he said to me, "Listen, do you think you can run this scene and show him how to run this scene?" I told him I probably could.

They took me inside to get all geared up and I ran the scene. Oliver went nuts. He's all over the place, saying, "That's what I'm talking about! That's what I'm talking about!" He looked at Michael Clarke Duncan and said, "You're fired. I'm going with him."

After that, the experience of being in that movie was great. We had a good time and it easily was the most fun movie to work in of all the movies I did. Part of that was because I was in my element. When I walk on the football field, hell, I'm at home. That was really fun. And the acting you have to do outside the football field—that was fun, too.

You look at Oliver's resume and he's done so many great movies like *Scarface, Platoon, Wall Street, Born on the Fourth of July, JFK,*

Natural Born Killers, and *Nixon*, to name a few.

Sometimes it was hard to get on the same page with Oliver. He'd try a lot of different things that didn't make sense until he found something that made sense. But he's a great guy. He has great vision.

The movie had a great cast that included Al Pacino, Cameron Diaz, Dennis Quaid, James Woods, Jamie Foxx, LL Cool J, Matthew Modine, Jim Brown, Lauren Holly, Ann-Margret, Aaron Eckhart, and Charlton Heston. Shit, he even had former NFL players play the opposing coaches. That list included Bob St. Clair, Y.A. Tittle, Pat Toomay, Dick Butkus, Warren Moon, and Johnny Unitas.

Working with Pacino really brought me a thrill, too. He'd been in some of the best movies of all time. I mean, the guy played Michael Corleone in *The Godfather*. It doesn't get much better than that.

In this one, Al played the old coach, Tony D'Amato, and I felt like I got a pretty good opportunity to get to know him. We would play cards and talk every day. But the biggest thing I remember about Al happened when it came time for that famous locker-room scene, the one they still play on all the scoreboards at football games today. He talks about fighting for inches, and how "we claw for that inch" and "we die for that inch." During the rehearsals for that scene, Al didn't seem to know his lines. He said things that he wasn't supposed to be saying and we were all wondering if he'd even looked at the script. A lot of us were going, "Man, this is going to take us forever to shoot this scene."

Then I learned what a professional Al is.

As soon as they said to roll the camera, that sumbitch went through that thing flawlessly. Everybody was like, "Get the f— out." We just went crazy, because we knew how well he'd done. The whole place felt like a pep rally scene. I mean, I thought I was playing football again. I couldn't believe it. He went through that thing so easily. Once they say "roll camera," that sumbitch knows what he's doing. I'm telling you—he was amazing. I promise you, during rehearsals, you would have said, "Man, this guy is going to ruin the picture." But, shit. What a professional. That guy knew what he was doing. That really taught me something.

I thought the movie was received well, though it received some criticism for not being realistic enough. There were some pretty far-fetched things, like the guy getting his eyeball torn out. Overall, I liked the movie, though, and, like I said, I really enjoyed acting in that film.

CHAPTER 5

GIANTS AFTER L.T.

by WILLIAM WYATT

SUPER BOWL XXXV

Ravens 34, Giants 7
January 28, 2001

The Giants were an unlikely participant in the big game, earning the franchise's third Super Bowl berth by virtue of a second-half hot streak that sent them back to Tampa, where they had won Super Bowl XXV 10 years earlier.

Head coach Jim Fassel's Giants improved to 12–4 in 2000 after going 7–9 the previous year.

How did they do it? They pretty much returned to the old-school recipe for winning football in the NFC East: they ran the football.

Ron Dayne and Tiki Barber gave the team a nice ground attack.

Dayne joined the Giants as their top pick in the 2000 NFL Draft. He'd won the Heisman Trophy in his senior season at Wisconsin and brought a smash-mouthed football component to the NFL. Dayne ran for 770 yards in his rookie season, which nicely complimented the quicker style of Tiki Barber, who came into his own in 2000.

Barber did it all that season. He ran the ball 213 times and gained 1,006 yards. He also scored eight touchdowns, caught 70 passes for 719 yards, and returned 44 punts for 506 yards and gained 266 yards returning kickoffs, giving him 2,497 total yards.

Kerry Collins returned as the team's starting quarterback after earning the job the previous season. The Penn State product had taken the Carolina Panthers to the 1996 NFC Championship Game, so he was no stranger to excellence. And he shined in 2000 when he completed 311 out of 529 passes for 3,610 yards and 22 touchdowns during the regular season.

Meanwhile, Michael Strahan served as the anchor of a strong Giants defense.

Strahan hung 9.5 sacks on the board while defensive tackle Keith Hamilton recorded 10. A strong defensive backfield composed of Emmanuel McDaniel, Shaun Williams, Jason Sehorn, and Reggie Stephens combined for 14 interceptions.

After 11 games, the Giants did not appear as though they would make the playoffs. They stood at 7–4 after losing to the Lions 31–21 on November 19. Later that week, Fassel guaranteed the Giants would make the playoffs. That's exactly what they did.

They won their final five regular season games to reach the mark of 12–4 and win the NFC East.

Once the playoffs began, the Giants stretched their winning streak to seven games with a 20–10 win over the Eagles and a 41–0 win over the Vikings in the NFC Championship game to reach the Super Bowl.

The Baltimore Ravens would be their opponent.

Led by linebacker Ray Lewis, the Ravens were a team known for an overpowering defense and a below-average offense. In their playoff wins over the Broncos, Titans, and Raiders, the Ravens allowed one touchdown and three field goals to become the seventh Wild Card team to reach the Super Bowl.

During the coin-toss ceremony prior to the game, the winners of the two previous Super Bowls in Tampa were honored. The Los Angeles Raiders won Super Bowl XVIII by defeating the Redskins. So Tom Flores, who coached that team, and the game's MVP, Marcus Allen, represented the Raiders. Meanwhile, the Giants, who won Super Bowl XXV, were represented by the the game's MVP, Ottis Anderson, and former Giants coach Bill Parcells.

Most forecast a defensive struggle and that's the direction the game appeared headed in the early going when the first five possessions of the game ended in punts. Receiving the fifth punt, Jermaine Lewis returned the ball 33 yards to the Giants' 31-yard line. After a holding penalty moved the ball back to the 41-yard line, Ravens quarterback Trent Dilfer connected with wide receiver Brandon Stokley for a 38-yard touchdown pass.

Sehorn, the Giants cornerback, got beat on the play, which came as no surprise given what had happened earlier in the action.

Ravens receiver Qadry Ismail had beaten Sehorn by 10 yards on the second play of the game. Dilfer's pass hit its mark, but what should have been a 59-yard touchdown turned into an incomplete pass when Ismail dropped the ball.

On the Ravens' second possession, Patrick Johnson had him beat along the sideline. Sehorn's luck again held true when Dilfer's pass missed him.

Sehorn's luck finally ran its course when Dilfer found Stokley.

Sehorn never caught up with Stokley when he broke free down the middle of the field.

"I can't blame it on anybody but myself; I got beat," Sehorn told the *Tampa Tribune.* "He made a great throw on the touchdown pass. He threw his best pass of the season in this game and it happened to be against me." He added: "Thank God [Dilfer] couldn't throw the ball that well. Or it would have been a lot worse."

Stokley's catch put the Ravens up 7–0.

The Ravens added a 47-yard Matt Stover field goal to take a 10–0 lead going into the half.

With 3:49 remaining in the third quarter, Ravens defensive back Duane Starks intercepted a Collins pass and returned it for a 49-yard touchdown to make it a 17–0 Ravens lead.

Ron Dixon answered for the Giants by returning the kickoff following Starks' score for a 97-yard touchdown to cut the Ravens' lead to 17–7. But that proved to be as close as the Giants would get the rest of the way.

Jermaine Lewis answered Dixon by returned the Giants' kickoff 84 yards for a touchdown to push the lead to 17 points.

The Ravens added 10 additional points while the Giants gained just one first down on their final four possessions and the Giants took their first Super Bowl loss in franchise history 34–7.

By winning, the Ravens became the third Wild Card team to win the Super Bowl and the second in four years.

All told, the Ravens' defense allowed just 152 total yards of offense. Included in the dominant performance were four sacks and five forced turnovers. Each of the Giants' 16 possessions ended with a punt or an interception.

Lewis became the second linebacker in Super Bowl history to be named MVP.

While the outcome of Super Bowl XXXV wasn't what Giants fans had hoped for, the run to get to that Super Bowl made the 2000 season special.

Super Bowl XLII

Giants 17, Patriots 14
February 3, 2008

Nobody forecast the Giants to go to the Super Bowl at the beginning of the 2007 season, much less reach the Super Bowl after they started with losses to Dallas and Green Bay in which they surrendered 70 points.

The team's fortunes got worse the next week against the Redskins at FedEx Field when they fell behind 17–3 at the half. Teams that start the season 0–3 don't typically go to Super Bowls.

Then something remarkable happened. A second-half rally featuring two 1-yard touchdown runs by Reuben Droughns tied the game at 17 before Eli Manning found Plaxico Burress for a 33-yard touchdown to give the Giants a 24–17 win.

Five additional wins followed. And by the time the Giants reached 10–5 heading into their final game of the regular season against the Patriots, they had the look of a team that might have something special going.

The Patriots entered the final week of the season with a 15–0 mark and had their eyes on breaking the 1972 Dolphins' record for excellence marked by a 17–0 season. Many had already ordained the 2007 Patriots as the NFL's all-time best, but they had to get through the

Giants to finish the regular season 16–0 and then win two playoff games and their fourth Super Bowl of the decade to reach exalted ground: 19–0.

Nobody could figure out how Giants coach Tom Coughlin would play the game. No matter what the outcome, they were locked into a playoff game the following week against Tampa Bay. Thus, many suggested the proper tack for Coughlin would be to rest his players so they could be well healed for the first round.

Coughlin chose the road less traveled and, ultimately, the Giants and he would be rewarded. Rather than rest the regulars, he played them and the Giants led 28–16 in the third quarter. But the Patriots came back to take a 38–35 win despite Eli Manning's four touchdowns and Domenik Hixon's 74-yard kickoff return for a touchdown in his first game as the Giants' kick returner.

Despite the loss, the game felt like a win. The Giants had gone toe-to-toe with the best team in football. What better way to boost a team's confidence entering the playoffs?

Afterward, Coughlin said: "There is nothing but positives. I told the players in playing this game everything would be positives, there would be no negatives, and that is how I feel. I don't know any better way to be prepared for the playoffs than to go against a team that was 15–0."

Once the playoffs began, the Giants became road warriors. They traveled to Tampa and came away 24–14 winners in their Wild Card matchup against the Bucs. Then they moved on to Dallas, where they beat the Cowboys 21–17 before finishing off the Packers 17–14 in overtime in the NFC Conference Championship at Green Bay. The win over the Packers had come in minus-23 degree temperatures. Lawrence Tynes came through on a game-winning 47-yard field goal after missing a 43-yard field goal in the fourth quarter and another with three seconds left in regulation to send the game into overtime.

Suddenly the Giants were in the Super Bowl against the undefeated Patriots. They had done so by winning 13 of their 17 games since starting the season 0–2. Needless to say, the Giants entered the game as huge underdogs in the minds of most, save for Burress, who predicted the Giants would overcome the 12-point spread to win the game. Coughlin wasn't amused by his receiver's prediction as he noted: "That's not what we aspire to do. We want to do our talking on the field. We've had a good theme all year long, which hasn't been that."

Included in that good theme was Manning, who continued his brilliance in the big game, throwing a game-winning 13-yard touchdown pass to Burress with just 35 seconds remaining to give the Giants a 17–14 win that seemed touched by the hand of God, or at the very least the hands of David Tyree.

After the Patriots forged ahead 14–10 with a 2:42 left in the game, the intrepid Manning completed five passes on the 83-yard go-ahead drive, which included a play that defied logic. Tyree hauled in a 32-yard pass by pressing the ball against his helmet and away from safety Rodney Harrison. After the catch, the Giants clearly seemed to have corned the market on karma.

The win gave the Giants franchise its third Super Bowl triumph in four Super Bowl appearances, giving them their sixth title game and seventh overall championship including the Super Bowl wins following the 1986, 1990, and 2007 seasons; NFL Championship Games in 1934, 1938, and 1956; and the league title in 1927, which came before a championship game had been born.

When the Giants returned home, more than a million fans showed up at Manhattan's Canyon of Heroes to salute their victorious team with a ticker-tape parade.

Topping off the 2007 season with a win in the Super Bowl easily ranked as the franchise's most improbable championship. They became just the fourth team to start a season 0–2 and reach the Super Bowl and the third to win it. On top of that, they won just three home games in 2007, marking the team as the first to have a losing record at home and still win a Super Bowl.

SUPER BOWL XLVI

February 5, 2012
Giants 21, Patriots 17

The 2011 Giants had a game-tested coach in Tom Coughlin, an experienced quarterback in Eli Manning, and a talent-laden roster. But few expected the team to amount to much in the tough NFC East.

Only the Giants appeared capable of changing that script.

With Eli Manning leading the way, they got off to a 6–2 start, running off big wins at Philadelphia—the Giants' first in the City of Brotherly Love since 2008—Arizona, and New England.

The Patriots game received billing as the rematch of Super Bowl XLII. Giants defenders were up to the task that day, picking off three Tom Brady passes. Turnovers were prevalent for both teams in a game that went down to the end.

Manning led the Giants on an 85-yard march that culminated with a 10-yard touchdown pass to Mario Manningham with 3:03 remaining to put the Giants ahead 17–13.

Brady then led a furious comeback. He found Rob Gronkowski on a 14-yard touchdown strike with 1:36 left in the game to give the Patriots a 20–17 lead. But Manning got back to work, leading his team 80 yards to the winning score, a 1-yard touchdown pass to Jake

Ballard with 15 seconds.

Following the 24–20 win over New England, the Giants encountered a rough patch that saw them lose five of their next six games to put them at 7–7 going into their final two games of the season.

The first of those games came against the Giants' crosstown rivals, the Jets, on Christmas Eve. The Jets needed to win their last two games to get into the playoffs, as did the Giants.

The Jets took an early 7–3 lead and had the Giants backed into a third-and-10 situation from their own 1. Manning found Victor Cruz on an out. After hauling in the pass, he broke two tackles and took off on a 99-yard touchdown jaunt.

The Giants rode the momentum created by Cruz's play to a 29–14 win, keeping their playoff hopes alive.

The Giants hosted the Cowboys on January 1, 2012. Because of the importance of the game—the winner would be the NFC East champion—the game got moved to prime time to be televised nationally.

Cruz again came up huge when he caught a 74-yard touchdown pass from Manning and the Giants held a 21–0 halftime lead. The Cowboys scored two unanswered touchdowns, but the Giants got a 28-yard field goal from Lawrence Tynes with 5:45 left and Hakeem Nicks caught a 4-yard touchdown with 3:41 left to put the game away for a 31–14 win.

The Giants were headed to the playoffs.

In order, they took care of the Falcons and Packers to reach the NFC Championship Game against the 49ers. The game went into overtime, where Tynes took care of business with a 31-yard field goal to send the Giants to Super Bowl XLVI.

Reaching the Super Bowl appeared to be an oddity since the Giants were the first team in NFL history to get there despite allowing more total points, 400, than they scored during the season, 394.

Once again the Giants faced the Patriots of Brady and Bill Belichick. Given the way their season had gone, the Patriots were once again installed as the favorites, as they had been in Super Bowl XLII.

Those who had paid attention to the Giants' run thought otherwise. They had evolved into a team that played a physical, tough, smart game without turnovers.

Brady struggled to put together drives throughout the game, which took place in Indianapolis. Meanwhile, the Giants pushed around the Patriots throughout the game, relying more on brute force and field position than anything fancy or tricky.

The Patriots were pinned in their own territory the entire game. Their own 29 would be the best starting position the Patriots would have to begin a drive for the length of the game. Three times they began drives from inside their own 10. That meant Brady and company had to cover a lot of ground on each possession to get to the Giants' end zone.

The first scoring play occurred when Giants safety Justin Tuck charged Brady and Brady threw away the ball and got busted for intentional grounding to give the Giants a safety and a 2–0 lead.

Cruz caught a two-yard touchdown from Manning with 3:24 left in the first quarter to push the Giants' lead to 9–0. The Patriots then made their charge.

Stephen Gostkowski kicked a 29-yard field goal and Danny Woodhead caught a 4-yard touchdown from Brady with 8 seconds left in the first half to give the Patriots a 10–9 lead. They added to the lead at the start of the second half when Aaron Hernandez caught a 12-yard touchdown pass from Brady, giving the Patriots a 17–9 lead.

Two Tynes field goals cut the lead to 17–15.

The Patriots then drove the ball onto the Giants' side of the field when Brady threw to Wes Welker, but the normally dependable receiver couldn't hang on to the deep pass. The Patriots were forced to punt, thereby setting up a Giants drive that would determine the outcome of the game and bring about one of the more controversial decisions in Super Bowl history.

During the regular season, Manning had led six comeback victories. He had also set an NFL record with 15 fourth-quarter touchdown passes. Now he had almost four minutes to try and make good on a seventh comeback victory.

On the first play of the drive, Manning threw a deep ball to Mario Manningham. Somehow he managed to make the over-the-shoulder catch just as he was pushed out of bounds. The 38-yard gain proved to be a healthy way to start the drive, putting the Giants at midfield with 3:39 left in the game.

Belichick challenged, but the officials upheld the call.

The Giants continued to advance the ball up the field until Ahmad Bradshaw burst through the middle of the line on second-and-6 with a minute to play. The ease with which Bradshaw went into the end zone made obvious the fact that the Patriots had chosen to let him score rather than let more time spill from the clock. Belichick obviously thought the only way they could win was to let the Giants score and get the ball back.

The Giants failed attempting a 2-point conversion to leave a 21–17 Giants lead on the scoreboard with 57 seconds remaining. Everybody in the football universe wondered at that point if the Giants had scored too quickly. Did Brady have enough time to take the Patriots the length of the field for a game-winning touchdown?

The final outcome came down to a Brady heave to the end zone on the last play. Rob Gronkowski almost came down with the pass before the ball dropped to the ground.

The Giants had a 21–17 win, the fourth in team history and Coughlin's second as coach of the Giants. Manning again won MVP honors, putting him in elite company. Prior to his winning the award for a second time, only four players in NFL history had won multiple Super Bowl MVP awards. That list included Brady, Bart Starr, Terry Bradshaw, and Joe Montana.

Manning did not seem too impressed by his award after the victory. "It's been a wild game, a wild season," he said. "This isn't about one person. It's about one team, a team coming together."

TIKI BARBER

Tiki Barber initially looked like he might be a nice piece for the Giants offense. He turned out to be so much more.

Barber and his twin brother, Ronde, both attended Virginia and were both drafted into the NFL in 1997. The Bucs selected Ronde in the third round, while the Giants picked Tiki in the second round.

Barber's first two seasons weren't anything special. He gained 511 yards and scored three touchdowns his rookie year in 1997. The 1998 season saw him gain just 166 yards in 52 carries and he followed that with 258 yards on 62 carries in 1999. Though the rushing yardage wasn't great, Barber established himself as a multiple threat that season with 1,639 all-purpose yards, including punt returns, kick returns, and receiving.

But 2000 became his true breakout season.

Barber gained 1006 yards on 213 carries with eight touchdowns and 2,497 all-purpose yards, becoming a big part of a Giants team that went 12–4 to win the NFC East Division and advance to the Super Bowl, where they lost to the Baltimore Ravens.

Barber again flourished the following season when he rushed for 865 yards and logged 1,802 all-purpose yards. In his final year of returning kicks in 2002, he accrued 1,989 yards while rushing for 1,387. The last game of the 2002 season, Barber gained 203 yards against the Eagles, who had one of the NFL's best defenses.

Excellence continued to follow.

From 2003 through 2006, Barber rushed for 1,216, 1,518, 1,860, and 1,662 yards. During that four-year period, he led the NFL in all-purpose yards in 2004 with 2,096, even though he no longer returned kicks. In 2005 he gained the most yards from scrimmage by any NFL running back. That same season he set the Giants' single-game rushing record when he ran for 220 yards against the Chiefs on December 17. Barber also broke loose for a 95-yard touchdown run against the Oakland Raiders in the final game of the 2005 season. That run set a team record for the longest touchdown run. Hap Moran had previously held the record with a 91-yard run against the Packers in 1930. Barber's jaunt came seven minutes into what would become a 30–21 Giants win. It also established the longest run ever against an Oakland team.

Along the way, Barber's peers voted him to three Pro Bowls.

Cutback running, quick feet, and being able to read the field were Barber's strong suits. However he did struggle hanging on to the football early in his career. He lost 12 fumbles in the 2002 and 2003 seasons. Giants coach Tom Coughlin stepped in to help Barber by teaching him to not hold the ball horizontally, rather vertically. Barber's fumbles lessened dramatically after the change.

Barber made the decision to retire at the end of the 2006 season, which he decided to announce in October. In making the announcement, he made public his intentions to begin a career in broadcasting. He also explained why someone at the peak of his career would retire by citing the physical demands of the game and how he wanted to leave the game in good health.

Barber put forth another stellar performance in his final season, particularly in the Giants' final regular season game when the team needed him most.

Playing an away game against the Redskins, the Giants needed a win to reach the playoffs. The Redskins were not having a good season, but the Giants entered the game having lost six of their previous seven games. Had the game been played at Giants Stadium, the chorus at the start of the game would have called for Coughlin to be handed his walking papers.

Fortunately for Coughlin and the Giants, Barber still had a little something left in the tank even though he planned to retire at the end of the season. Barber came through with the best game of his 10-year NFL career.

Barber scored three touchdowns and ran for 234 yards—breaking his own Giants single-game rushing record—in a 34–28 win that put the Giants into the playoffs, giving the team its first back-to-back appearances since 1989–1990. Barber's touchdowns included runs of 15 yards; 55 yards; and, finally, a 50-yard scamper with 6:13 remaining that saw him cut to the left, break a tackle, and sprint to the end zone to give the Giants a 13-point lead and put the game away. He set a single-game record for the most yards gained by a player over 30 years old.

The following week, the Giants faced the Eagles in Philadelphia in a Wild Card game that turned out to be Barber's finale, as the Eagles won 23–20.

Barber did not go gently into that good night, running for 137 yards in the losing effort.

After the game, Eagles players paid tribute to Barber.

Linebacker Jeremiah Trotter noted: "I just told him that I loved him and good luck in his second career and that it's been great going against him."

Eagles safety Brian Dawkins told Barber: "You're a warrior."

Later, Dawkins said, "I've always said that I respect that dude. That will never change.... A lot of people have written him off time and time again on what he couldn't do. He runs hard; he's hard to bring down; and week in, week out, those guys can count on him."

Barber allowed that Dawkins' sentiments "meant a lot to me."

"That's his mentality of how he plays the game and it made me feel good," Barber said.

Though the standout Giants running back decided to cash in his chips before being a part of a winning Super Bowl team, he noted that not winning a Super Bowl would not define him.

"My legacy will be of someone who has played through the ups and downs and good times and bad, and you always knew what you were getting out of me on Sunday," Barber said. "I have never given up. I have never walked off that field without leaving it all on the field."

Ironically, the season following Barber's retirement, the Giants advanced to Super Bowl XLII and pulled an upset over the 18–0 Patriots to claim the franchise's third Super Bowl win.

Barber finished his career with a team-record 17,357 total yards. Of that total, he gained 10,449 yards rushing. And his 55 rushing touchdowns were the most in team history.

ODELL BECKHAM JR.

Odell Beckham Jr. joined the Giants in 2014 when they selected him out of LSU in the first round with the 12th pick of the NFL Draft.

When a team has a quarterback like Eli Manning, they typically want him to have quality receivers to throw to and Beckham looked to be that guy. Ironically, Beckham already had a tie-in with the Manning family. He attended high school at Isidore Newman School in New Orleans, the same high school where each of Archie Manning's sons—Peyton, Eli, and Cooper—attended. During Beckham's senior year he caught 50 passes for 19 touchdowns and 1,010 yards, pairing him with Cooper Manning as the only players in Newman school history to exceed 1,000 receiving yards in a season.

Once at LSU, Beckham started nine of the Tigers' 14 games as a freshman. By his junior season, most regarded him as one of the best receivers in the country when he finished the season with 57 catches for 1,117 yards and eight touchdowns. Given that background, the Giants couldn't resist selecting him when his name remained on the board when their turn to pick arrived.

A hamstring injury delayed the start of Beckham's rookie season with the Giants, but when the time came for his Giants debut, he opened with a bang on October 5, 2014, against the Atlanta Falcons.

He caught four passes for 44 yards and a touchdown.

While insiders recognized what a key addition Beckham was for the Giants, a national audience began to appreciate his abilities after watching him during a *Sunday Night Football* game on November 23, 2014, when he caught 10 passes for 146 yards including two touchdowns. But the one-handed touchdown catch he made in the second quarter of the Giants' 31–28 loss to the Cowboys brought him his most recognition.

Eli Manning arched a pass to the end zone and Beckham stretched backward. With his body fully extended and Cowboys cornerback Brandon Carr draped all over him, he used his right hand to reach as far as possible while Carr grabbed his jersey. Beckham battled back, appearing to pin Carr's arm while pushing him away before making the 43-yard touchdown catch. Beckham's ability to stay in bounds made the play all the more special.

Two penalty flags were thrown. Had Beckham interfered with Carr or vice versa? Officials identified Carr as the offender on the play.

Replays confirmed that Beckham had remained in-bounds.

Beckham noted that he concentrated only on catching the ball rather than worry about keeping his feet in-bounds or fending off Carr. The rookie receiver complimented his quarterback, saying that Manning's pass "couldn't have been placed better."

"It was a perfect spiral," Beckham said. "With a ball like that, it makes it a lot easier to make a catch."

Beckham impressed Manning by being able to maintain control of the ball without pulling it into his body for security.

"It was like he caught it with a couple of fingers," Manning said. "It also looked like he pulled it down and was ready to throw it. He kind of had a grip on it like he was ready to make a throw."

Making one-handed catches is always at the front of Beckham's mind. He forever practiced making one-handed catches at practices and before games as far back as his days at LSU. With the Giants he practiced with Giants equipment man Ed Skiba tossing spirals to him.

Beckham's incredible catch birthed a new Twitter hashtag: #ThingsOdellCouldCatch. And social media began to blow up with the question: Had Beckham just made the best catch ever?

The Pro Football Hall of Fame certainly thought so, since they put on display Beckham's jersey from the night he made his one-handed grab.

Another highlight from Beckham's rookie season came when he caught 12 passes for 140 yards with three touchdowns on December 14, 2014, against the Redskins. That performance tied former Giants tight end Mark Bavaro's team record for most catches in a single game.

Beckham capped his amazing rookie season with 12 receptions for 185 yards and a touchdown against the Eagles, setting a club record for most receiving yards in a game by a rookie.

Beckham finished the season with 91 receptions for 1,305 yards and 12 touchdowns in 12 games.

After the season, the Pro Football Writers named him the NFL Offensive Rookie of the Year, as did the Associated Press. Beckham also ranked highly in regard to pop culture, which led to his selection as the player to grace the cover of *Madden NFL 16*.

During the week leading up to the 2015 Super Bowl, Beckham—the man synonymous with the one-handed catch—teamed up with New Orleans Saints quarterback Drew Brees to set a world record for the most one-handed catches made in a minute by catching 33. That record later got broken by Andy Fantuz, a Canadian Football League player, who caught 50.

Beckham's rookie excellence carried over into his second season with the Giants in 2015, when he caught 96 passes for 1,450 yards and 13 touchdowns.

Great things are expected from Beckham in the future as his Giants career unfolds.

ELI MANNING

I've been asked a lot whether I think Eli Manning plays the quarterback position better than Phil Simms played it during his prime. Well, I don't even want to compare him to Phil Simms. Phil was one of the best quarterbacks of my era; he was tough, talented, and knew what he was doing. But Eli has impressed me. He stands tall in the pocket and throws the ball without showing any fear. —L.T.

Talk about the pressure of having to fill big shoes. Few in sports have ever faced the pressure staring down Eli Manning.

With Archie Manning as a father, Eli faced the prospect of living up to a legendary college quarterback who turned out to be a standout in the NFL. If that wasn't enough, big brother Peyton Manning managed to be equally jaw-dropping in college as well as an All-Pro NFL quarterback.

Unlike Peyton, who attended the University of Tennessee, Eli dared to play his college ball at his father's alma mater, Ole Miss, immediately facing the scrutiny of alumni who remembered when Archie became arguably the best player in the school's storied history. And somehow Eli managed to deliver.

Eli's career numbers showed 10,119 passing yards and 81 touchdown passes while he earned a 137.7 passer rating. In the process, he established or tied 45 records. That led to a third-place finish for the Heisman Trophy and a truckload of other accolades. Primary among those was that of the NFL, which deemed him as the best quarterback in the 2004 NFL Draft. Accordingly, the San Diego Chargers selected him with the first overall pick, despite Eli's declaration that he would not play for the Chargers. Manning's days as a Charger were shortened to minutes when they traded him to the Giants, who sent back Philip Rivers and draft picks to the Chargers for Manning.

In other words, Eli Manning fit the bill. More challenges and accomplishments would come with the Giants.

But greatness could be seen from the get-go, despite the 0.0 passer rating he earned in his fourth start, December 12, 2004, against the Ravens in Baltimore. Manning earned a seat on the bench for the second half, but he remained the Giants' starter, and he began the 2005 season as the Giants' starter. He seemed to turn the corner during a loss to the Chargers in San Diego on September 25, 2005. Chargers fans feeling spurned by Manning booed him throughout the game. Though the Giants lost 45–23, Manning delivered a 24-for-41 performance good for 352 yards and two touchdowns.

The next week he threw for four touchdowns at Giants Stadium in a 44–24 win. He finished the season in the top five for passing yards and touchdown passes, leading the 11–5 Giants to an NFC East crown and a spot in the playoffs where they bowed out via a 23–0 first-round loss to the Carolina Panthers.

Manning again played splendidly while leading the Giants to the playoffs in 2006, but once again they lost, this time in a close one 23–20 to the Philadelphia Eagles.

The frustration of making the playoffs in consecutive seasons and bowing out in the first round served as an inspiration for what would take place during a special 2007 season.

Manning remained in New York over the offseason leading up

to the 2007 season, refining his game while working with Giants coaches and receivers in the hopes of reaching a common goal.

As if a precursor for what sat ahead on the horizon, Manning showed off his improved stature against the Dallas Cowboys in the season opener, throwing for 312 yards while completing 28-of-41 passes for four touchdowns and an interception. Unfortunately for Manning and the Giants, he left the game with a shoulder strain. That would be the first in a series of challenges Manning faced that season, including one delivered by John Mara, who questioned Manning's leadership. The Giants' co-owner was quoted in the *New York Daily News* after he said: "The only thing we evaluate is, 'Can we win with this guy?' That's the one thing. When we talk about any player at the end of the season, the No. 1 question is, 'Will he help us win?' And to take it one step further, 'Can we win a championship with this guy?'"

Manning continued to struggle right up until the final game of the season against the undefeated New England Patriots. Even though the Giants lost 38–35 and the Patriots moved to 16–0, Manning showed well by throwing four touchdowns. And perhaps even more important, he played well enough to gain the right mindset for facing the Patriots.

Manning and the Giants began their playoff march with a 24–14 win over the Tampa Bay Buccaneers en route to another matchup with the Cowboys, who were the top seed in the NFC.

Once again the Giants prevailed with Manning leading the way to earn a spot against the Green Bay Packers in the NFC Championship Game on January 20, 2008. The Giants managed to take a 23–20 win in overtime to earn a spot in Super Bowl XLII.

Manning completed the magical season by leading the Giants to a 17–14 win over the undefeated Patriots, who entered the game as 12.5-point favorites. The late-fourth-quarter drive Manning led proved pivotal in the victory and also earned him MVP honors.

Manning would again lead the Giants to a victory in Super Bowl XLVI against the same Patriots and once again, he earned MVP honors.

Yes, Eli Manning has big shoes to fill, and has gone so far as to outgrow those shoes during his illustrious time as the Giants' quarterback.

JIM FASSEL

I didn't think Jim Fassel deserved to get fired as the Giants'
coach when he did. If you're a coach and you're fired,
they're basically telling everybody you're a bad coach. He
wasn't a bad coach. But I don't believe there was anything
left he could do with the team. When a team thinks you
can't go any further with a guy, you have to make a deci-
sion. So the Giants decided he had to go. Sometimes you
just need a change of coaches to keep things fresh, too. Any
coach only has so many speeches. Everybody gets too com-
fortable if the same coach sticks around too long. But Jim
Fassel did some good things while he was the coach of the
Giants.—L.T.

Giants fans will forever remember Jim Fassel as the coach who
figured out a way to rally the troops for a memorable run to the
Super Bowl in 2000.

The Giants named Fassel the 16th head coach in team history prior
to the 1997 season. Even though Ray Handley and Dan Reeves had
served stints as the Giants' coach after Bill Parcells, his immense
shadow still loomed over the franchise. Following Parcells was like
being the Yankees' right fielder following Babe Ruth. And buzzard's
luck put an ironic twist on Fassel's first year: Parcells returned to New

York to coach the Jets that year.

Fassel made a few mistakes, but the Giants made great strides in his first season, none of them more apparent than a change in the team's attitude.

Danny Kanell started 12 games at quarterback and, under Fassel's direction, took a conservative approach by managing the game and minimizing mistakes. And he employed three capable running backs in Tiki Barber, Tyrone Wheatley, and Rodney Hampton. But the biggest difference from the previous year's team was the defensive line, a unit that had been thought of as the weakest link of the team's defense. Michael Strahan greatly aided that effort by leading the team with 14 sacks and 89 quarterback pressures, and was in on 49 tackles.

That added up to a turnaround that saw the Giants improve from 6–10 to 10–5–1, which earned a berth in the playoffs as the NFC East champions. But they bowed out of the playoffs in spectacular fashion against the Vikings.

Playing in sleet and snow at Giants Stadium, the Giants led 22–14 at the two-minute warning against a team that had fumbled four times and dropped four passes. And the Giants' defense had stuffed the Vikings' offense all week, as evidenced by their standout running back Robert Smith's meager 40 yards on 16 carries.

But quarterback Randall Cunningham found Jake Reed for a 30-yard touchdown before Chris Calloway misplayed the Vikings' onside kick to give the Vikings the ball at their own 39 with 1:25 remaining in the game. From there, the Vikings drove deep into Giants territory to set up Eddie Murray's game-winning 24-yard field goal that quieted a crowd of 77,497.

Though the season ended on a disappointing note, Fassel was recognized as Coach of the Year by the Associated Press, *Pro Football Weekly*, *The Sporting News*, and United Press International.

Fassel's Giants went 8–8 in 1998 before losing the final three games of the 1999 season to finish at 7–9 and out of the playoffs. Those seasons led to his defining moment as coach of the Giants.

After going 7–2 to start the 2000 season, the Giants took back-to-back losses to the St. Louis Rams and Detroit Lions. Days after the Lions loss, Fassell employed an unprecedented tack.

With five games left in the season and his team standing at 7–4, Fassel stepped forward and guaranteed that his team would make the playoffs.

Fassel told reporters the following at his weekly press conference: "You got the laser, you can put it right on my chest; I'll take full responsibility. I'm raising the stakes right now. This is a poker game, I'm shoving my chips to the middle of the table, I'm raising the ante, anybody wants in, get in, anybody wants out can get out. This team is going to the playoffs, OK? This team is going to the playoffs. Wellington Mara made a statement to me when I took this job that I'll always remember. He said, 'This is not an easy job. If it's an easy job you wouldn't have it.'"

Fassel did not appear to be speaking out of emotion; rather, he sounded like a man who had put some thought into what he planned to say then let it out. During his talk, Fassel continuously stated that his team was playoff bound and he equated the final five games of the season to, among other things, driving a bus, boarding a train, a poker game, and a horse race.

In the aftermath Fassel's guarantee, the Giants went on a five-game winning streak to close the season at 10–6 and make the playoffs as the NFC East champions. They continued their winning ways in the playoffs, defeating the Eagles 20–10 at Giants Stadium before destroying the Vikings 41–10 to advance to the Super Bowl, where they lost to the Baltimore Ravens 34–7.

Fassel's Giants went 7–9 the season after their Super Bowl run, then finished 10–6 in 2002 to reach the playoffs. Unfortunately for Fassel and the Giants, they blew a 24-point lead against the 49ers with four minutes left in the game and lost 39–38 to get bounced from the playoffs.

When the Giants got off to a bad start in 2003, the whispers about

Fassel's job security began to intensify. Week 7 saw the Eagles defeat the Giants 14–10 when Brian Westbrook returned a punt 84 yards for a touchdown. In Week 9, the Giants took a 31–28 overtime win over the Jets to move to 4–4 on the season with the one-win Falcons visiting Giants Stadium the following week. But the Falcons routed the men in blue that afternoon 27–7, erasing any semblance of momentum.

After the Saints defeated the Giants 45–7 in New Orleans in the Giants' 14th game, Fassel requested a meeting with Giants owners Bob Tisch and Wellington Mara. Sensing that they were going to fire him, he asked them to go ahead and announce his dismissal. After the announcement that came that he would no longer coach the team, Fassel coached the final two games of the season, which the Giants lost to finish 4–12.

Fassel finished with a 58–53 record as the Giants' coach, taking the Giants to the playoffs in three of his seven seasons.

TOM COUGHLIN

I never knew Tom Coughlin when he coached for the Giants and I was a player. The simple explanation for that is that he was an offensive coach. No reason for him to talk to me. I mean, I knew who he was and would maybe speak to him. But if I'm talking to a coach, I promise you it's not some-body from the offense. I'm talking to the head coach or the defensive coordinator.

I didn't know him like that. I couldn't even tell you what years he coached with the Giants. I just didn't know. That's one of the funny aspects about being on a football team, particularly an NFL team. Everybody thinks because I was on such-and-such team during the same time as somebody else, that we know each other. That's not the way it is.

I knew basically everybody from the defense. We'd sit in the room together all day. I especially knew the guys on the defensive line and the linebackers. The linebackers hung with their group, but we also hung with the defensive line, because we're all entwined right there. And I knew all the defensive coaches. I would have regular contact with the linebackers coach and the defensive-line coach. I probably had less contact with the secondary coach. The secondary coach, you're going to know him, but not like that, because the secondary hangs in their own little group. But the secondary is probably the most foreign on that defense. I can't even remember who most of the secondary coaches were when I played, much less the offensive coaches.—L.T.

Who says that an old dog can't learn new tricks?

A man once thought incapable of humor and a perpetual hard-ass, Tom Coughlin did some self-examination and decided to lighten up. The change played a key role in how the Giants resurrected their team under him and won two Super Bowls.

Coughlin became coach of the Giants when he replaced Jim Fassel in January 2004 after Fassel's team went 4–12 in 2003. Coughlin brought with him a broad resume that included being the first head coach of the Jacksonville Jaguars, Boston College head coach, and a stint as the Giants' wide-receivers coach under Bill Parcells.

Coughlin could obviously coach. He knew Xs and Os as well as technique. Take Tiki Barber's fumbling problem. From the 2000 season through 2004, the Giants' star running back coughed the ball up 19 times. Coughlin taught Barber a different technique for holding the football and the results were immediate, as Barber fumbled just once in 2005. That decrease allowed Coughlin to call Barber's number more often and his production increased dramatically.

Still, Coughlin's results were mediocre, and New York is not a good place to be mediocre. After seasons of 6–10, 11–5, and 8–8 records, Coughlin entered the 2007 season with a 25–23 mark and on the hot seat. But Coughlin didn't need to watch the news to understand he had a problem. The 8–8 record in 2006 alerted Coughlin to the fact that his rough edge might not play well with the players, who remained the same age while he grew older. So he opted to change his ways. Without going soft, he just chose to show a more human side. Remember, Coughlin was a guy who was so gung-ho and military-like in how he ran things that he didn't even allow his coaches to wear sunglasses when he coached the Jaguars.

"Colonel Coughlin" essentially giving himself a make-over prior to the 2007 season and his willingness to do so paid off immediately.

The 2007 team presented a major challenge for Coughlin as Barber retired. Ironically, one of the reasons he cited for retiring at the peak of his career was Coughlin's hard-ass practices.

Coughlin didn't have to stray far to find Barber's replacement.

Brandon Jacobs, who had spent two years on the roster, became the guy. Despite fighting injuries, the hard-running Jacobs managed to rush for 1009 yards in 2007.

One thing Coughlin didn't have to worry about was the quarterback position. Eli Manning returned to start his fourth season with the team and threw for 3,336 yards and 21 touchdowns to lead the Giants to a 10–6 season.

Of all the regular season games the Giants played, their loss in the final game of the 2007 season might have been the most significant in pointing them in the right direction. That's because they went against the New England Patriots, a team one win away from a 16–0 season. The Giants were already in the playoffs, but Coughlin opted to play the game straight up to preserve the integrity of the game. While the Giants lost 38–35, Coughlin's move to bang with the AFC's best team turned out to be a brilliant long-term move. Afterward, Giants players realized that the Tom Brady–led Patriots were indeed mortal.

The Giants moved through the playoffs to earn the NFC's spot in the Super Bowl, where they met the Patriots, who were hoping to become the first undefeated NFL team since the 1972 Miami Dolphins.

On February 3, 2008, the Giants met the Patriots at University of Phoenix Stadium in Glendale, Arizona. Despite entering the game as 12-point underdogs, the Giants came away with a 17–14, come-from-behind, upset win in Super Bowl XLII.

Afterward, a smiling Coughlin told the media: "The best part of it for me is the idea that this group of young men came together and believed in themselves, bought the team concept completely, took the names off the back of the jerseys, checked the egos at the door."

And why wouldn't the Giants players buy in? Their coach had made a move to grow. And that move changed the whole dynamic of the team.

Coughlin's Giants enjoyed modest success from 2008 through 2010, but that did not improve the team's outlook during a struggle-filled 2011 season that saw them win three of their last four games to finish 9–7 and win the NFC East.

The Giants' hot play continued, earning them a spot in Super Bowl XLVI, where they met the 13–3 Patriots. Once again the Giants found themselves in an underdog role and once again the Coughlin-coached Giants defeated the Patriots 20–17 to claim the Giants' fourth Super Bowl.

Coughlin resigned after the 2015 season, his 12th as coach of the club. He said of his decision: "I strongly believe the time is right for me and my family, and…the Giants organization.…This is not a sad occasion for me."

In 20 NFL seasons, including eight with the Jaguars, Coughlin's team's compiled a 182–157 record in regular and postseason games. His Giants teams went 113–98.

SOURCES

Newspapers
The Buffalo News
Austin American-Statesman
Florida Times-Union
Chicago Tribune
Associated Press
The *New York Times*
The (Hackensack, NJ) *Record*
Boston Herald
Cincinnati Enquirer
St. Louis Post-Dispatch
Saginaw News
Detroit News
The Daily News
Herald News (Woodland Park, NJ)
Jackson Citizen Patriot (MI)
New York Post
St. Paul Pioneer-Press
Hartford Courant
Staten Island Advance

Websites
Michiganlive.com
USAToday.com
NewJersey.com
ESPN.com

Buscema, Dave. *100 Things Giants Fans Should Know & Do Before They Die.* Triumph Books: Chicago, 2012.

Carson, Harry. *Point of Attack: The Defense Strikes Back.* McGraw-Hill: New York, 1986.

Maxymuk, John. *The 50 Greatest Plays in New York Giants Football History.* Triumph Books: Chicago, 2008.

ABOUT THE AUTHOR

Lawrence Taylor is a Hall of Fame linebacker who spent 13 seasons, his entire professional career, with the New York Giants. He was second in all-time career sacks at his retirement, was the NFL Defensive Player of the Year three times, and earned 10 Pro Bowls. He lives near Miami, Florida.